# HUMILITY

# HUMILITY

*Rediscovering the Way of Love and Life in Christ*

Michael W. Austin

WILLIAM B. EERDMANS PUBLISHING COMPANY

GRAND RAPIDS, MICHIGAN

Wm. B. Eerdmans Publishing Co.
4035 Park East Court SE, Grand Rapids, Michigan 49546
www.eerdmans.com

Published 2024

Book design by Lydia Hall

Printed in the United States of America

30  29  28  27  26  25  24      1  2  3  4  5  6  7

ISBN 978-0-8028-8210-3

**Library of Congress Cataloging-in-Publication Data**

A catalog record for this book is available from the Library
of Congress.

*This book is dedicated with gratitude and love to*
*Jeff Acton, Andrew Cromwell, and Jeff Silva,*
*friends on the Way.*

# Contents

# *Foreword*

It has become clear that we live in a time when many Christians have indeed lost their way—and lost contact with *the* Way.

Certain things that used to be able to be taken more or less for granted no longer can be taken for granted. One of these is the centrality of Jesus for Christianity. Another is the centrality of character for Christians, both in personal morality and in what we look for in political and cultural leaders.

Doctrinal weaknesses on the liberal Christian side have been visible for a long while. The danger there has been a version of the gospel watered down to little more than liberal verities and progressive politics.

But a more recent development on the conservative Christian side has been the encroachment of culture-wars tribalism and its apotheosis in #MAGAvangelical Trumpism.

If the goal of "Christian" people becomes winning the culture wars against the liberals, at all costs, with people like Donald Trump as role models, this project requires a remaking of Christian identity, with the biblical Jesus and biblical standards of Christian character as casualties.

In this book, Michael Austin humbly and lovingly teaches us about the Christian virtues of humility and love. He calls for a rediscovery of this way of living, which he rightly identifies with the Way of Jesus Christ. Humility and love, along with other core virtues discussed here, clearly characterized Jesus's way of living, and also the way he taught his disciples to live. These virtues were consistently reinforced in the rest of the New Testament—this is one of the most significant points of continuity in the New Testament.

Austin lets us in on old debates in Christian theological ethics over subtle questions related to (a) the actual possibility of Christians making positive strides in moral growth and becoming manifestly better people, and (b) the relative significance of human moral effort versus divine forgiveness, and (c) the role of the Holy Spirit in bringing heart- and life-change to believers.

These debates reflect older confessional differences that remain with us today. For example, a certain kind of Lutheran-Calvinist Reformational vision is pessimistic about how much Christians should expect moral growth to occur and doubts whether it is a good thing to shift Christian focus off grace as forgiveness to grace as empowerment for growth. Certainly, this vision does not support the development of a theology in which the church is understood as a community of the holy rather than a community of sinners saved by grace. The danger here, however, is just what Austin recognizes—too ready a surrender to unholiness, too low an expectation of Christian virtue.

The Wesleyan tradition demurs from this pessimism and emphasizes growth in holiness, or sanctification, as a fundamental aspect of Christian theology and ethics. Christians are expected to undertake earnest efforts to become more like Jesus. Similarly, the Anabaptist tradition developed a vision of the church as a set-apart community of believers working hard together and against the primary currents of culture to follow the Way of Jesus Christ in their daily lives. The danger here can be a navel-gazing moral perfectionism, whether individualist or communal, but in light of the deterioration of "Christian" morality in the United States today it is hardly the most serious worry that we face.

So three cheers for Michael Austin's effort to help American Christians in particular to rediscover the Way of Jesus Christ. We need to meet Jesus again, as if for the first time. His humility and love are a great place to start.

*David P. Gushee*

# Acknowledgments

I'm grateful for family, friends, mentors, colleagues, and others who had a part in this book. Several people read portions of an early draft. Thanks to Dawn Austin, Teena Blackburn, Josh Crawford, Andrew Cromwell, and Travis Stephens for taking the time to do so, and for their feedback.

I'd also like to express my thanks to everyone at Eerdmans. This is my third book with them, and I have enjoyed our partnership once again. Thanks to Trevor Thompson, James Ernest, Lydia Hall, Jason Pearson, Jennifer Hoffman, Sarah Gombis, and the many others at Eerdmans who helped get this book out into the world. Thanks as well to David Gushee for taking the time to write the foreword and capturing the heart behind this book.

Parts of chapters 2, 3, and 6 are drawn from material originally published in my book *Humility and Human Flourishing* and have been reproduced by permission of Oxford University Press (https://global.oup.com /academic/product/humility-and-human-flourishing -9780198830221).

Finally, I'd like to offer a heartfelt word of thanks to my wife, Dawn. She, more than anyone, has taught me what humility and love look like in the reality of everyday life for followers of the Way.

one

# The Neglected Way

We've lost our way. Instead of allowing God to lead us in paths of righteousness for his name's sake, we've too often followed a different way, our own way. The earliest Christians were known as followers of the Way.[1] But we've taken lesser paths, paths that divert us from the Way. For millennia, the paths of power, pleasure, and wealth have been powerfully seductive paths that lead many astray. They remain so today. In recent years, the lesser path of partisan politics on the left and the right has been especially attractive to many in the United States. Other lesser paths lead us, we hope, to comfort, respect, or self-optimization.

All of these paths lead us astray. They can seem like they might be the Way. God wants us to enjoy life, doesn't he? We can use the power and wealth we gain to do good, right? God does want us to enjoy life, to use the power we have for good, to enjoy the good gifts he gives, and to share generously. But often our good intentions fall short. Rather than receiving joy from God, we devote ourselves to comfort or even outright hedonism. We often coat our pursuit of power, pleasure, and wealth with a Christian veneer, but what is underneath is not truly Christian, because it is not truly Christlike. Many of us have taken what we thought was the Way of Christ, a path we are told will please God and therefore bring us happiness, success, and other blessings. We are told, sometimes explicitly, sometimes implicitly, that if we just read our Bibles enough, pray enough, serve our church (and maybe our community) enough, give away enough money, then life will pretty much go as we want it to. We'll be fulfilled, feel close to God, be part of a good church, have a happy marriage and family, experience deep friendship, and find fulfillment in our career.

With all this in mind, we follow this path. But if we are honest, we have discovered that this path doesn't lead us to where we want to be, nor where we ought to be. We don't have the kind of fulfillment we thought we'd have. God often seems absent at best and uncaring at worst. We question whether God is even real. We are frustrated with church. Our marriages bring disappointment, both in ourselves and in our spouses. Some marriages barely survive, while others don't make it at all. Our kids break our hearts, in small and large ways. We do the same to them. They wander away from the faith or pursue a life of faith very different from our own that we don't understand. We wonder what, if anything, we could have done differently to keep them on what we think is the right path. Friends disappoint us. We disappoint them. And the time we spend working can seem futile.

There is no easy solution here. The world, the church, and we human beings who inhabit them are fallen.

Things in the world, in the church, and in us are not what they are supposed to be. God feels distant. Community with our siblings in Christ at church takes work and seems elusive. Marriage is hard. So is singleness. If we have children, they become adults who ultimately make their own decisions, for better or worse. Deep friendship seems unattainable. And at its best work is still work.

Yet in the midst of the pain, suffering, disappointment, and frustrations that mark our time on this planet, there are also green shoots of truth, goodness, beauty, and unity. Sometimes they grow and even flourish. Creation is being redeemed; we play a part in that (Rom. 8:18–25). We receive many good gifts from God in this fallen world: God himself, the body of Christ, deep friendship, a vocation, and perhaps marriage and parenthood. We won't get everything we want. Even so, we can experience shalom and help others do the same. Shalom is, very simply, a deep inner well-being, inner harmony, and wholeness. It includes harmony with others, with the rest of creation, and with God.[2] Shalom will not come about without God's transformative activity in our lives, in our relationships, and in the world. God must work. Yet we have a part to play here, too, a part that is often neglected.

## The Revolution of the Way

What is it that we need, as followers of the Way, in order to play our part in God's redemptive story? God, obviously. Fellowship with Christ and community with others who seek to love and follow him, certainly. Character, clearly. Character plays a key role in our relationship with God, our relationships with others, and doing our part to usher in God's kingdom.

Character matters. We see this truth in the character of those who have done heroic things, especially those who have been martyrs for Christ. We rightly honor those who have sacrificed their lives for Jesus. Several years ago, I took a trip to London that drove home the sacrifices made by several Christian martyrs. I was invited to give a talk on developing character in sports at the Royal Institute of Philosophy. I'd been to London once before, but I was excited to go share my ideas and see the city again. Plus, the trip was paid for, which isn't something that happens to philosophy professors very often! My wife, Dawn, was able to join me, so we took in some of the sites and experiences London has to offer: Parliament, the Tower Bridge, Buckingham Palace, an open-air shopping market in Chelsea, fish and chips at a London pub, cider and ale at another London pub, and an Arsenal match at the Emirates Stadium. We also visited Westminster Abbey, where I had an unexpected experience that I think about to this day.

Before our visit to the abbey, I didn't know about the ten statues above the Great West Door commemorating twentieth-century martyrs.[3] Such people obviously have shown true greatness of character. We should admire them for how they lived and for their willingness to die for their faith. We should admire Dietrich Bonhoeffer's opposition to Hitler and the Nazis. We should admire Oscar Romero's defense of the poor and opposition to a ruthlessly violent dictatorship in El Salvador. We should admire Esther John's devotion to sharing the gospel while teaching women to read and working alongside them in the cotton fields of Pakistan. We should admire Martin Luther King Jr.'s persistent nonviolent struggle for racial equality and justice. We should do more than admire them. We should let them inspire us to do what we can to make the world a better place, to serve God and our fellow human beings in humility and love.

It's unlikely that we will face the kind of choices these and other martyrs did. But character matters for us, too. It matters for us as members of a church. It matters for us in friendship, in family, and in our work. It matters for us in the daily interactions we have with God, with other people, and in how we steward all that God has given us. It matters for us on social media, in how we interact with each other there and in person. It matters for us in politics and political conversations.

Christians past and present testify that character is central to what it means to be a Christian. In a discussion of Colossians 3:5–14, Rebecca Konyndyk DeYoung puts it this way: "*the* moral project for a Christian is to die to the old self and rise to new life in Christ."[4] C. S. Lewis puts the same point succinctly, straightforwardly, and memorably, as he so often does: "Every Christian is to become a little Christ. The whole purpose of becoming a Christian is simply nothing else."[5] DeYoung is right. We must die to ourselves and live for Christ. Lewis is right. To become a Christian is to become like Christ. To become a little Christ is to be like him in all of life. This change in us will likely be slow. Even very slow. We shouldn't focus on achieving the elusive goal of perfection. But we should be moving toward becoming a little Christ. We should be making progress. This should be the overall orientation of how we live as followers of the Way.

What does it mean, though, to be a follower of the Way? What does it mean to become like Christ in *all* of life? Dallas Willard explains, "as a disciple of Jesus I am with him, by choice and by grace, learning from him how to live in the kingdom of God. . . . I am learning from Jesus to live *my* life as he would live my life if he were I. . . . I am learning from Jesus how to lead *my* life, my *whole* life, my real life."[6] For my life, this means that I should seek to be the husband, father, friend, professor, member of Covenant Community Church, high school soccer coach, writer, activist, and citizen that Jesus would be if he were I. This is a tall order, and it's not even a comprehensive list. But what greater purpose, what greater vision for our lives, could there be? In order to make progress in such a way of life, we must be growing in the virtues of Christ. It's essential. Our character must increasingly reflect his character.

Character should matter to us for many reasons, but primarily because it matters to God. Willard is helpful again: "The revolution of Jesus is . . . a revolution of *character*, which proceeds by changing people from the inside through ongoing personal relationship to God in Christ and one another. It is one that changes their ideas, beliefs, feelings, and habits of choice, as well as their bodily tendencies and social relations. It penetrates to the deepest layers of their soul."[7]

This book focuses on the roles of humility and love

in transforming our character, our relationships, and the world. This really can happen as we allow these realities to penetrate to the deepest layers of our souls and spread throughout our communities. This is the revolution of the Way of Jesus. The revolution of the Way does not involve coercion, mere political power, violence, social status, or any of the other traits of lesser revolutions. The revolution of the Way is different. It's a revolution of character and community, a revolution of humility and love.

## The Neglect of Character

In recent years, talk about character has increased, yet character itself is neglected in many ways. Character was often discussed in the run-up to the 2016 presidential election and continued throughout the presidency of Donald Trump. As white evangelicals (broadly conceived) overwhelmingly voted for and then continued to support President Trump, many in and out of the church were confused. Others were angered. Still others defended their support of Donald Trump. Part of the confusion and anger could be traced back to the 1990s. During this time evangelicals were, well, evangelistic about character. Many criticized Bill Clinton for his behavior with Monica Lewinsky. The refrain was, "If you can't trust him to stay true to his marriage vows, how can you trust him to be president?" During this Clinton scandal, the Southern Baptist Convention was unequivocal in the stance it took. The SBC rejected the idea that Clinton's immoral behavior should be tolerated as long there is economic prosperity. It warned that "tolerance of serious wrong by leaders sears the conscience of the culture, spawns unrestrained immorality and lawlessness in the society, and surely results in God's judgment" and further stated that "moral character matters to God and should matter to all citizens, especially God's people, when choosing public leaders . . . we implore our government leaders to live by the highest standards of morality both in their private actions and in their public duties, and thereby serve as models of moral excellence and character . . . we urge all Americans to embrace and act on the conviction that character does count in public office, and to elect those officials and candidates who, although imperfect, demonstrate consistent honesty, moral purity and the highest character."[8]

Character counts, until it doesn't. Such double-mindedness can be found across the political spectrum. Perhaps it has always been so, but these days it seems worse. For many, as long as someone belongs to their political tribe, they are willing to overlook offenses that would draw instant condemnation when committed by political opponents. We should be concerned about the character of our political leaders, and there are difficult questions to work through as we balance the stated positions of a candidate with concerns, if there are any, over that person's character. I'm convinced that a certain minimum standard of character is required for any leadership position, political or otherwise. Consider the fact that if a person has bad enough character, it's not reasonable to trust them to do what they say they will do. A candidate for mayor or president might tick all of your preferred policy boxes, but what reason do you have for thinking that they will actually be true to their word? If they lack integrity, you have very little reason to trust them. Doing so is risky. You might get what you want, but the odds are against it. And there are, as we've seen, other costs as well.

The neglect of character is not just a political issue. It is also a personal and social one. Not only is character often neglected; it is sometimes even ignored. This happens in our homes, churches, and local communities. We should be concerned about the character of other leaders, too, not just in the political realm. The president's character matters, but so does the character of your child's soccer coach. In many ways the coach's character matters more, given their direct influence on your child. And, obviously, your own character matters. So does mine.

Apart from our own experiences, what evidence do we have that character is neglected? There is a large body of research from the past sixty years or so on the state of our character.[9] While the results are mixed, they reveal serious problems. For example, many of the hundreds of studies done by psychologists show that most people will not help others, even when doing so would be fairly easy. This is true in small everyday situations, like helping someone who has dropped a stack of papers. We are much more likely to help when there is an emergency, though this is not the case if we are in a group of strangers. In those cases, we most likely will refuse to help because we fear embarrassing ourselves somehow. Research also shows that most people are willing to do terrible things to others if someone they see as an authority figure is pressuring them to do so, even if they won't be punished for refusing. And most of us are willing to cheat in academics, finances, sports, and other realms of life. There is also evidence that people lie to others in about one-third of our interactions with each other. We humans have a character problem.

A recent survey of Christians provides evidence that we have a character problem.[10] Seventy-two percent of practicing Christians completely or somewhat agreed with the statement "To be fulfilled in life, you should pursue the things you desire most." Sixty-seven percent of practicing Christians also completely or somewhat agreed that "The highest goal in life is to enjoy it as much as possible." Such beliefs, if put into practice, undermine good character. The first one assumes that there is no such thing as a bad desire, if it is something we desire the most. But that's not true, as experience, reflection, and the Bible all testify (see Col. 3:5–11). If I accept that my highest goal in life should be to enjoy it as much as possible, I naturally adopt a self-centered approach to life. Such an approach is antithetical to the teachings of Christ. What sort of character is formed in me if enjoyment is my highest goal in life? Not a virtuous one, to be sure. Imagine how this belief would impact my relationships with others in my family, my friends, and my fellow Christians at church. Yet a majority of practicing American Christians apparently agree with these claims. What we believe is not all that matters. We are also creatures of emotion and desire. Our actions are influenced by belief and desire; both are influential. Both must be attended to, then, as we seek to grow in Christ.

Christians should be concerned about our character.

We should be especially concerned about the character of leaders in the church, given their influence on the rest of us and the responsibilities they have. Good character—not perfect, but good—should be a nonnegotiable for pastors, elders, Sunday school teachers, small group leaders, church boards, ministry leaders, and others who have influence in and beyond our congregations. Yet Christian leader after Christian leader has their credibility rightfully destroyed by their acute hypocrisy and immorality.

I remember my shock several years ago when an influential person in Christian publishing told me that the virtue language in the New Testament is *merely* aspirational. That is, Christians shouldn't really expect to make much, if any, significant moral progress in this life. But this attitude is alien to the New Testament writers, who speak of being transformed (Rom. 12), of being a new creation (2 Cor. 5:17; Col. 3), and of a life that reflects the very character of God (2 Pet. 1:3–11). It is also refuted by the experience of those who have been transformed by their union with Christ through his Spirit in his church. But if we believe that there isn't really any hope of change, is it any wonder that the lure of influence, power, pleasure, or wealth overtakes any concerns certain leaders have about character and true faithfulness to Christ? Is it any wonder that these and other concerns capture not just the hearts of many leaders but ours as well?

It's not enough to merely say we value character or to desire it in ourselves and others. Nor is it enough to bemoan its absence in the church and in the world. Action is required. We need to do something. We can do something.

We can cultivate character as we pursue a transformational relationship with Christ in a like-minded community of fellow disciples. As we will see, the virtues of humility and love play a vital role in this transformation.

## Cultivating Character in Christ

At some level, most of us know that character matters. We look around us and see the neglect. We look inside of ourselves and see the neglect. But we also feel a bit hopeless. We find it hard to believe that things can be different than they are, that we can be different than we are, better than we are. We certainly want to avoid a misguided zeal about ethics and character. We are right to be concerned about this. Yet in my experience there is also a significant and perhaps growing antipathy toward ethics among some that I find alarming. For example, former *Christianity Today* editor Mark Galli addressed the seriousness of ethics in a column entitled "Mastering the Golf Swing of Life."[11] From the title, you might think that an ethic of imitation, of practice, and of sustained effort will be the focus. But the subtitle points in a different direction: "We tend to think of ethics as real serious business. It is not." Galli points out that PGA golfers will tell you that in a round of golf where they hit two under par, there are maybe two out of seventy shots that were hit "exactly as they intended them." This is the nature of golf. According to Galli, it is the nature of life as well. As he puts it, "the sooner you come to grips with incessant failure, the more you can enjoy the game."

There are several issues here to consider. First, *must*

we accept incessant failure in the Christian life? Second, *should* we accept incessant failure in the Christian life? Third, *how* is enjoying life related to failure and to having good character?

Galli is right that growth requires grace and that we are unable to attain perfection both on the golf course and in the spiritual life. Yet he's mistaken about some pretty important things.

First, he's pessimistic about our potential to be radically transformed in this life. Galli thinks most of the language about such transformation in the New Testament is *anticipatory*. That is, he believes it has more to do with our life in Christ at the end of the age, when all is ultimately redeemed and transformed. Until then, "we muddle along mired in sin, but not without hope." The good news is that this does not define us. Forgiveness, grace, and God's love define us.

Thankfully we are defined in the deepest ways by divine forgiveness, grace, and love. But there is great potential for deep moral and spiritual transformation in the here and now. Our hope is not just for transformation in the next phase of life. Our hope includes deep change in this life. That is also part of the good news of God's kingdom. This will be a recurring theme of this book, but I encourage interested readers to explore for themselves several key passages in the New Testament to determine whether or not Galli is correct. I'm convinced that a careful reading of Romans 12, 2 Peter 1, Galatians 5, Ephesians 4–6, Colossians 3, and the Sermon on the Mount tells us that there is hope for deep transformation *in this life*.

Second, Galli states that "we are in the bad habit of

thinking that ethics is REAL SERIOUS BUSINESS, that our welfare and the welfare of the world depend on its proper execution. Not quite. The gospel is the end of ethics in this sense. . . . The welfare of the world is a settled issue." In one sense, Galli is right. The *ultimate* welfare of the world is a settled issue, but the welfare of the world between now and the redemption of all things is not settled, and this is why ethics *is* very serious business. To put it another way, I'm glad that individuals such as William Wilberforce, Dietrich Bonhoeffer, and Sojourner Truth took ethics seriously. We ought to do the same.

Our welfare in this life ultimately depends upon God. But we have also been given the freedom and the power to impact it for better or worse. If I am open to the fullness of God's Spirit and growing in love, joy, peace, patience, kindness, goodness, faithfulness, gentleness, and self-control, my life will be better for it. We cannot make ourselves better. Yet we can and must work in partnership with God, becoming more like Christ in this life, sometimes in radically transformative ways. It is also clear that this sort of life is better and more enjoyable for us than a life of hate, sadness, anxiety, impatience, cruelty, badness, unfaithfulness, arrogance, rudeness, and a lack of self-control.

Not only will our lives be better as we grow in virtue; we can help make the world better, too. We can have an effect on the welfare of the world, in a variety of ways. If we are cultivating and practicing compassion, then there will be less suffering in the world. Surely we fall short, but the regrettable state of the world should move us to seek to grow in this and other Christian virtues. Followers of Jesus have played and continue to play important roles in expanding literacy, providing health care, abolishing slavery, fighting human trafficking, battling racism and misogyny, serving women in crisis pregnancies, and countering many other social injustices. Christians have failed in many ways, and we could contribute more, much more, to the common good. Nevertheless, the welfare of the world does depend on ethics, which makes it very serious business indeed. Ethics, and in particular good character, must be given the place it deserves in the life of the follower of Christ and in Christ's body, the church.

Cultivating character is nonnegotiable for anyone who is serious about following Jesus Christ. The ancient Greeks believed that if you wanted to become a better person, to grow in virtue, it was mostly up to you. You had to work at it. Aristotle gives voice to this belief when he asserts that "we become just by doing just actions, temperate by doing temperate actions, brave by doing brave actions."[12] Fortunately, we are not left on our own to grow in virtue. That's not to say that we don't need to do something. As Dallas Willard helpfully observes, "Grace is opposed to earning, but it is not opposed to effort."[13] We are transformed by God's Spirit and by working with God in a variety of ways. The spiritual disciplines, including deep involvement in a Christian community, offer the context for our efforts to grow, grounded in God's grace and love.

One important concern about an emphasis on cultivating character is that it can seem like it reduces Christianity to a moral self-help or self-improvement project.

The Gravity Leadership Podcast, one of my favorites, gives voice to this concern. They have several central principles that are important for Christian leaders, and really anyone seeking to be a disciple of Jesus. One of these principles is that *the goal of our discipleship is not moral perfection or cognitive certitude; the goal of discipleship is divine union.*[14]

In their discussion of this principle, one of the hosts—Ben Sternke—shared a lesson he learned many years ago as a parent. He shared that having kids helped him see clearly that he simply was not a good person. When his kids wouldn't do what he said, when he felt disrespected, a real darkness in his heart was revealed. At the time, Ben says, he had an arrangement with God: if you follow the rules, God will bless you. But he kept losing it with his kids, and this drove him away from God to fix himself. After trying to figure things out and do just that, he'd come back to God and convince himself that everything was okay. This led him to experience deep guilt and shame about who he was. He came to realize that his lack of faithfulness could be swallowed up by God, that union with God was possible. And Ben realized that he "didn't need to be a good boy to get it." There is no contract with God that if we are good, then God owes us something. This approach can actually cut us off from God. But we follow a God of grace and truth, who wants union with us just as we are, in all of our imperfection, sin, and darkness. He's not waiting for us to become morally perfect so we can be united to him; he offers us union now, just as we are. Augustine discusses this very temptation. He says that those who believe in "do-it-yourself purification . . . who think that they can purify themselves for contemplating God and cleaving to him by their own power and strength of character . . . are thoroughly defiled by pride."[15] Once we realize this is a temptation, rather than a truth, we'll be a little further on our way to deeper union with God.

I had an experience similar to Ben's. I remember thinking as a young single guy just out of college that I was pretty unselfish. I know, I know, but I was twenty-one and had been a Christian for about four years, so just bear with me. I thought I was unselfish. Then I got married. A whole new depth of selfishness and pride in my heart was revealed. I made some progress and grew just a little bit as I sought to love my wife more than myself. Then we had our first child. Then our second. Then our third. Our three daughters are some of the most important gifts from God to us. I'm grateful to be their dad. But to this day, I come face-to-face with the pride and darkness in my heart as I seek to love them as Jesus does. It's not because of anything they do; it's because I've got a long way to go in becoming more like Jesus, in taking on his character in my heart and life.

The goal of discipleship is not intellectual certainty or moral perfection. It is union with God. God isn't waiting for us to become morally perfect so we can be united to him. He offers that union to us now, just as we are. *But union with God is itself morally transformative.* As we go further up and deeper in, we will be changed. Our character will grow. We'll still be fallen, still far from perfect. But we will be changed. How could it be otherwise, as we more deeply know and experience the God who is, in his very essence, love?

We can focus too much on character or approach the journey of character development in ways that are unhealthy. But if we realize that union with God changes us, and if we work with God in grace and truth toward such change, it will happen. We'll become more like Jesus, and we'll experience him and his love more deeply.

So character not only matters; it can also be cultivated. We can change. Really. And we must do so. Really. But how do we do this? How do we become like him? In particular, how do we reflect his humility and love? We'll explore these questions more in the pages to come, but in short, we must be with Jesus. Not only must we be with him, but we must do so in a particular way. We must be with Jesus with this as a central focus: *"to learn from him how to be like him."*[16] When we do this, we discover that Jesus's inner life was nurtured by how he spent time with his Father. In the New Testament, we find evidence of Jesus practicing and teaching about numerous spiritual disciplines: studying God's word, prayer, solitude, silence, fasting, service, celebration, and fellowship. These and the other disciplines of the spiritual life that he practiced can be practiced by us as well. They must be if we are to be more like him, if we are to become little Christs. We can do this only by God's grace. But we have to do something, engaging in these practices as a means of opening ourselves up to grace. You must make your heart available to God through the spiritual disciplines, so that "Christ is formed in you" (Gal. 4:19). So must I. So must we all.

We can make genuine progress. We really can become more like Jesus. But what does it mean to become more like

Jesus, to cultivate Christlike character? It means that we cultivate virtue, including the virtues of humility and love.

But what exactly is a virtue? A virtue is simply a moral habit, a character trait. It is an excellence of character, one that helps us live well and be fully human. For instance, someone who has the virtue of honesty will be disposed to perform honest actions, to speak the truth even when it is difficult. Their beliefs, emotions, desires, and dispositions ground their honest words. The same can be said of other virtues, like courage, compassion, humility, and love. As we grow in these virtues, we become the kind of people for whom virtuous actions become second nature.

We aren't left on our own to grow in virtue. The same power that raised Jesus from the dead is available for our own moral and spiritual transformation (Rom. 6:4; 8:11). We are to be "transformed" by the renewing of our minds (Rom. 12:1–2). That same Greek term is rendered as "transfigured" in Matthew 17. Think of the difference in the physical appearance of Jesus as he was transfigured before Peter, James, and John. The profound difference signified in the transfiguration points to a profound change in our transformation as described in Romans 12:1–2. Certainly we will fall short. We will stumble and fall. But we can also make significant progress as we work with God in dependence upon grace and the Holy Spirit to become more like Christ. We *can* make progress. But are we? I'm afraid that, too often, the answer is no.

There are many reasons for this. Perhaps we don't really want to change. I'm sure Marlena Graves is right when she observes that "we ignore the way of Jesus because it is inconvenient or because we are too busy or because our ultimate allegiance is found elsewhere."[17] There are other reasons, too. Perhaps we don't know how to change. Or perhaps we believe cultivating Christlikeness is a passive process, not involving anything we *do*. But think about it. Think about the teachings from Scripture that tell us we have a role to play in our moral and spiritual growth. In Colossians 3 we are told to *set* our hearts and minds on Christ. We're taught to *put* our earthly nature to death and to *rid* ourselves of such evils as rage, malice, and slander. We're taught that we must *put on* Christ, *put on* the new self, and *clothe ourselves* with virtue. In 2 Peter 1, we're taught to *make every effort* to grow in faith, goodness, knowledge, self-control, endurance, godliness, mutual affection, and love. We aren't left to do this on our own, but our own efforts are needed.

Another essential element of cultivating character in Christ is community. In his book *Life Together*, Dietrich Bonhoeffer—German theologian, pastor, and martyr at the hands of the Nazis—offers a rich discussion of life in a Christian community.[18] It is in our relationships with other Christians, in particular those who are physically present in our lives, that we are able to experience the transforming presence of the Trinity. The presence of fellow Christians is a physical sign of God's presence with us. For Bonhoeffer, life in community is a gift, a grace for which we can be thankful.

Our growth does not depend solely on us but also on the church. I must admit, when I first realized that I needed other people for my growth in Christ, I didn't like it. Perhaps it was the American ideal of individualism I'd imbibed for decades. Perhaps it was also a bit of pride and a desire to be self-sufficient. Likely, it was (and is) all of these.

In the past couple of years, God has answered a long-standing prayer of my wife, Dawn, and me. We are part of a community of people who not only talk about community but seek to live it out in very tangible ways. This is something we've longed for but just haven't been able to find. There is an authenticity to our community that we enjoy and for which we're grateful. It's a young church plant, and there will be issues, challenges, conflict, and the like, but also resolution, restoration, and unity.

Our church is focusing on a particular area of our town and asking people to move there. We recently did just that. This has included plenty of frustration, as we moved from a house that was built twenty years ago and didn't need much work at all to one that is nearly a century old. A leaky basement and the need for a host of new things—HVAC units, a roof, gutters, wiring, plumbing, and probably some things I don't know about at the moment—have all brought to mind something a friend of mine likes to say: "Why be happy when you can be a homeowner?" But we are grateful, too, for the house and what we hope it will become: a beautiful place where people will come and experience grace and the love of Christ. We're also grateful for where this home places us in our town and church community. Friends from church live across the street and around the corner. We see them regularly. They even stop by unannounced! Many others live nearby. One of the significant things about this is that it offers multiple opportunities for growth together in Christ, as we encourage each other, bother each other, forgive each other, and love each other.

There is something significant about physical proximity that makes a difference, a real and substantial difference, not only for our life together with other Christians but also for sharing that life with others who live in the downtown area that is a focus of our church's ministry. Recently, I put an old bathroom vanity out on the sidewalk to be hauled away. A day or two later, I noticed someone trying to attach the vanity top to his shopping cart with strips of fabric. I had the sense I should initiate with him, maybe help him, but I hesitated. After seeing him still struggling with it a few minutes later, I found some rope and went outside, offering it to him. He said, "You're four minutes too late!" I told him to keep the rope in case he could use it in the future. We had a short conversation, and before I knew it he was sharing about his wife who had died due to complications from disease, and then a girlfriend who was murdered. I didn't do much besides listen and express my sorrow for what he'd endured. At the end he apologized for dumping his troubles on me, but of course I didn't mind and told him I was glad he did. I hope to see him again.

As I've begun to accept the truth that I need others to grow in Christ and that they need me, and as I've made a bit of progress at living this out, I'm grateful for all of it. I'm grateful for others who play a part in helping me grow. I'm also grateful to play a part in doing the same for them. I'm grateful for a ten-minute conversation with a guy who had a use for our old bathroom vanity. We need each other.

That's the way God made us. Rather than resisting it, we should embrace it. We can't cultivate character alone.

## Rediscovering the Way

Humility and love are essential for good character. These virtues are two essential parts of the Way that we must re-discover and re-place at the center of our lives and our life together. Many of the basic truths about character we've just discussed are also true of humility and love. These two Christian virtues matter. They've been neglected, but they can be cultivated and must be cultivated. Community plays a key role in cultivating them. They are crucial for flourishing in Christ. They are vital for experiencing shalom and helping others do so as well. And we need God's help if we are to grow in these virtues.

While they have not been completely abandoned, humility and love are often overlooked, undervalued, and even disregarded. We've lost our way. We've lost the Way. Pride and hatred show up where humility and love are desperately needed. These virtues are crucial for fol-lowing Jesus. They are crucial for being like Jesus. They deepen our union with Jesus. They are part of what it means to be a follower of the Way of Jesus. They are vi-tal for extending the blessings of the Way to our friends, family, community, and a world in desperate need of truth, beauty, goodness, and unity. The more that follow-ers of Jesus live out the virtues of humility and love, the more the church will become the life-giving community it can be. We need these virtues and all the good things they bring.

My hope is that this book can play a part in helping us rediscover the importance of these virtues and experience the goodness they bring to our lives and the lives of others. We can rediscover the Way if we truly follow the one who is the Way. We can show others the Way, not merely tell them about it. Humility and love are essential for this. We need Christ to show us what these virtues are, to help us grow in them, and to give us the strength to be humble and loving in whatever circumstances come our way. We can rediscover them—we must rediscover them—if we are to be faithful to the prayer Jesus taught his disciples in Matthew 6:10:

> Your kingdom come.
> Your will be done,
> on earth as it is in heaven.

Let's turn our attention to the character of Jesus, to his humility and love, and set our hearts and minds on making progress on the Way.

two

# *Rediscovering Christ's Way*

I was recently searching online for artwork depicting Jesus washing the feet of his disciples. Some of what I found was a little kitschy for my taste. Some of it was terrible. But I also found several artistic renditions that capture something of the beauty, goodness, humility, and love of Christ in their depictions of John 13:1–17. I recommend taking a few minutes and doing this yourself. Find a few visual depictions of this passage that are especially meaningful to you, that draw you into what Jesus does here. Maybe one captures the humanity of Jesus. Maybe another really shines a light on his humility or love. Maybe you will be struck by what this must have been like for his disciples, perhaps feeling some of their discomfort. Once you find one or two that speak to you, take several minutes and meditate on them, with heart and mind open to what God might teach you through the experience. Then return here, as we examine the Scriptures to see what they reveal to us about the humility and love of Jesus.

The Bible gives us a rich understanding of the virtues of humility and love. The humility of Christ is on display all over the Scriptures. The washing of the disciples' feet is one excellent example. We'll zero in on Philippians 2:1–11, where Paul describes some of what Christ gave up for the good of the world. The self-emptying of Christ is set forth as a pattern for his followers not just to admire but also to imitate. We'll see that humble human beings are like the humble Christ, putting the interests of others ahead of their own. As we do this, we'll "shine like stars in the world" (Phil. 2:15), giving people a small taste of the character of Jesus and the kingdom of God, something the world desperately needs.

The unconditional love of Christ is evident throughout the gospels and the rest of the New Testament. His love for the Father and all of humanity runs through it all. This gracious and extravagant love is famously described in 1 Corinthians 13. These two passages, Philippians 2:1–11 and 1 Corinthians 13, have much to teach us about humility and love. They form the heart of the scriptural basis for the rest of this book.

We're going to dig into these two passages a bit. This work is important, first, as it helps us better understand the character of Christ, especially his humility and love. It's also important because seeking such understanding is a way of loving God with our heart, soul, mind, and strength. Third, this work is worth our time and effort because our beliefs matter, a lot. They aren't all that matters. Our desires, emotions, and will are all vital, too. But the challenge of being loving and humble, in the way that Jesus exemplifies, can be very difficult. This difficulty demands that we have the Spirit-empowered strength of deep convictions, of strongly held beliefs that help shape who we are and how we live, if we are to grow in humility and love.

The aims of this chapter are simple, then. We're going to take a deeper look at the humility and love of Jesus Christ, who is the Way and shows us the Way of humility and love, with the ultimate goals of knowing him more deeply and growing to be more like him.

## The Humility of Christ

Humility is a misunderstood virtue. Much of what passes for humility is not humility but something else. Humility can also be hard to find. It seems rare. It might be fashionable to talk about and praise humility, but how many shining examples of it have we actually seen? We are all too often influenced by our anxious desires for power, pleasure, and wealth, rather than being filled with the peace and generosity that humility produces.

But there is one in whom humility positively shines. The Bible testifies to the humility of Christ in many places. The washing of the disciples' feet is one well-known example. Jesus, who is our "Lord and Teacher," does this for his disciples and tells them they ought to do the same for others. Taking the humble posture of a servant, performing an act of service that was seen as low and demeaning, is a beautiful example of humility. It is an example we, his followers, are to imitate (John 13:14–15). Jesus says that he is "humble in heart" (Matt. 11:29). He claims that true greatness in the kingdom of God comes not from wealth, social status, or power. Rather, it comes from humility (Matt. 18:1–5). Luke starts off his gospel portraying Jesus with the outcasts, the lowly, and the poor, and as the son of an unmarried young woman. In so doing, "Luke sets up his basic theme that, coming out of Israel's history, Jesus is the universal bearer of burdens, concerned especially for women, the poor and outcasts, of all nations and races."[1] Such people were considered outcasts in this culture, but Jesus ignores that and treats them not only with respect but with humility and love.

The central New Testament passage on the humility of Christ is Philippians 2:1–11. We won't examine every verse in this passage. Entire books have been written about parts of it. But we will dig in at some key points.[2]

To understand this passage in context, let's first look at the main idea of Philippians, found in 1:27: "live your life in a manner worthy of the gospel of Christ." The subsequent verses describe what this means. A life that is worthy of the gospel is a life of unity, courage, faith, and suffering for Christ (1:27–30). A literal translation of "live your life" is "live out your citizenship."[3] The idea is that the members of the Philippian church are part of a new society, a new commonwealth, where Jesus rather than Caesar is Lord. Roman citizens didn't think of humility as a virtue, but rather as something to be avoided. Followers of the Way were to be different. More specifically, they were to display a countercultural character, one in which humility plays a central role. We should do the same today. Just as they proclaimed by their words and their lives that Jesus is Lord, not Caesar, so should we. We should proclaim that Jesus, not (insert your favorite politician or political party here), is Lord by our words, our actions, and our very being.

With this in mind, let's look at Philippians 2:1–11:

If then there is any encouragement in Christ, any consolation from love, any sharing in the Spirit, any compassion and sympathy, make my joy complete: be of the same mind, having the same love, being in full accord and of one mind. Do nothing from selfish ambition or conceit, but in humility regard others as better than yourselves. Let each of you look not to your own interests, but to the interests of others. Let the same mind be in you that was in Christ Jesus,

> who, though he was in the form of God,
> did not regard equality with God as some-
>     thing to be exploited,
> but emptied himself,
> taking the form of a slave,
> being born in human likeness.
> And being found in human form,
> he humbled himself
> and became obedient to the point
>     of death—
> even death on a cross.
> Therefore God also highly exalted him
> and gave him the name
> that is above every name,
> so that at the name of Jesus
> every knee should bend,
> in heaven and on earth and under the earth,

and every tongue should confess
that Jesus Christ is Lord,
to the glory of God the Father.

The term translated as "humility" in this passage is a rich one. If we understand it in the overall context of Philippians, we can get a clearer picture of the humility of Christ and its relevance for us. Humility has to do with our attitude toward both ourselves and others. It has to do with acting for the good of others. What does it mean to "regard others as better than yourselves"? It means that we are to put their interests ahead of our own, as Christ did for us. In the Roman culture at Philippi, where honor was highly prized, these attitudes and actions would have been highly unusual. They remain so today, for a variety of reasons.

Human nature being what it is, such humble sacrifice is not the norm. Our first impulse is often to do what we can to climb the social ladder at work, at church, or in our community. But Paul is instructing the Philippians to be different. They aren't to climb the social ladder. Neither are we. Instead, we are to move down the ladder and serve others.[4] What might this look like for you? It depends. For some, this would mean intentionally serving your LGBTQ+ neighbor in humble love. For others, it might mean intentionally serving your white Christian nationalist neighbor in humble love. For some, it could mean engaging your neighbor with a "Black Lives Matter" sign in their yard in humble love. For others, it could mean doing the same with your neighbor who has an "All Lives Matter" sign up in theirs. But for all of us, it means we are ready to serve our neighbors, whoever they are, and whatever they believe, in humble love. That humble love may look very different, depending on our neighbor and our context, but it is nonnegotiable for followers of Christ.

Paul recognizes that our selfish ambition and conceit often stand in the way of our humble descent into service. We want to prop ourselves up. We want to climb the social hierarchy. We want to be over others, standing above them on the ladder of power or prestige. We want to be thought of highly, to get the honor and respect we believe we deserve. This is sadly true in the church, where the lust for prestige and power can rear its head in especially ugly ways. Many of us unfortunately use church to work out a lot of our issues. We may not feel we are the friend, spouse, or employee that we want to be. We don't get our emotional needs met by our friends, by our spouse (if we are married), or by others at work. Because of this, we turn to church to get those needs met. We think if we can "succeed" at church, then everything will be okay. This can lead to grasping for power, prestige, or respect inside the body of Christ. If we feel a lack of these things at home, with friends, or at work, then church becomes a place we can pursue them. Some really odd social hierarchies can pop up in church, where much dysfunction is present. Sometimes, it leads not only to dysfunction but to truly evil behaviors, including exploitation, manipulation, and various kinds of abuse. None of this should be tolerated. Toleration of such evil is not the Way of Jesus. Ever.

As followers of the Way, we have many good reasons to humbly serve others. One important reason is discussed in this passage from Philippians. Jesus chose to forgo the power and prestige that are rightly his as the Son of God. He stepped down the ladder—*way* down—and became human. But he didn't just become human, though that exemplifies great humility in and of itself. He became human and was obedient to the point of a humiliating death on a cross. Our familiarity with this story as Christians doesn't breed contempt, as the saying goes, but it can produce indifference, apathy, and a lack of gratitude. We must humble ourselves before these truths—the true story of the incarnation, crucifixion, and resurrection—realizing not only the greatness of the story but the greatness of the God at its center. Familiarity can be a barrier to this. We must not let it be so.

To live a life worthy of the gospel necessitates that we embrace this humility of Jesus, imitating him in ways that make sense in our lives. We exemplify humility in how we care for others. Rather than holding tightly to what he had a right to as the Son of God, he "did not regard equality with God as something to be exploited, but emptied himself, taking the form of a slave." We must also refuse to hold tightly to the many things that hold us back: power, prestige, wealth, comfort, and social acceptance, not to mention anger, malice, pride, and hatred. Jesus of course had no sin to hold him back, but we do. We must be willing to relinquish our sin and vice, but also many good things, if we are called to do so. Jesus gave up so much for us. Paul, following Jesus's example, gave up some of his rights for the sake of the gospel (1 Cor. 9:15). We might be called to do the same. It may not be easy, but it will, ultimately, be good.

Jesus humbly sacrificed so much for us, but we resist following in his steps. Jesus did this for us, yet we bristle at *that person* getting recognition at church, when so much of what *we've done* goes unrecognized. Jesus did this for us, but we focus on *getting what we want* out of friendship or marriage, rather than taking some time to focus on what *we might give* to others. Jesus did this for us, yet we bristle at the thought that someone else might have a different political perspective than our own, *just as grounded in their faith* as we believe ours to be. Jesus did this for us, yet we bristle at the idea that someone else's health and well-being is more important than our alleged rights *during a global pandemic*. Jesus did this for us so that we could do the same for others: sacrifice whatever God asks us to sacrifice, in order to help bring about the humble, loving, and just community of the kingdom of God. In this community, the humble and loving communion of the Trinity is at the center. We are not at the center. God is.

But there is a humility that keeps us at the center of our little universe. This counterfeit humility can often flourish in churches and other Christian settings. Think of the person who simply will not accept a compliment, for even the smallest of things, as if doing so is an affront to God. This might seem like humility, but it isn't. It is a convoluted way of making oneself the center: "I do not deserve this compliment . . . I am doing better than I deserve . . . I am a horrible sinner and do nothing good on *my* own." Perhaps these responses are true. I'm sure they are sometimes sincere, and other times not. But in my experience they sometimes seem like convoluted strategies for expressing an ultimately false humility. I'm not blaming anyone for this. Some of us are confused about humility. Some of us aren't sure what to do with a compliment, or how to avoid pride when we are good at something or have done something admirable. Sometimes the mark of humility in response to a compliment is simple gratitude, and then silence. When we make a show of our "humility" and unworthiness, we make a show about us. That's not humility.

True humility is not easy. The truly humble person recognizes that all the good they possess is a gift from God. They graciously accept a compliment, and perhaps also say a silent prayer of gratitude in response to it. They don't feel the need to run themselves down as a little show of false humility that in essence is a form of pride, a form of drawing attention to *their* "spirituality" and *their* "humility." As C. S. Lewis rightly observes, "a really humble man . . . will not be thinking about humility: he will not be thinking about himself at all."[5] The humble life is centered neither on ourselves nor on our humility. It is centered on God. The natural result is a humility that puts the interests of others ahead of our own.

If we seek to put the interests of others ahead of our own, in humility, we imitate the good and beautiful example of Jesus. We also prepare ourselves for what life in the kingdom will be like in the new creation, when all is made right, with humility and love at the center of it all. We get a foretaste of that kingdom now, in our own little communities, in our own little lives. Not only that, but we make that foretaste available to others, offering them a sample of the overwhelming goodness of God and life in his kingdom.

What is the person like who follows Christ in his humility? The humble person fights to descend the social ladder, rather than climb it. The humble person makes the interests of others their priority, rather than their own. Instead of always grasping for what they want, the humble person serves others, for their good, often in sacrificial ways. The humble person focuses on God and others, rather than themselves. The humble person is steeped in the love of God, and that love flows from God through them to others. To better understand that kind of love, let's take a look at one of the most beautiful and challenging passages in all of Scripture.

### The Love of Christ

Back when all three of our daughters were younger and living at home, there were times when the daily grind of life seemed, in many ways, futile. I remember feeling this really deeply one night, standing at our kitchen sink, washing the dishes. Unlike Brother Lawrence, who wrote of practicing God's presence and finding joy in Christ while cleaning pots and pans in the kitchen of his medieval monastery, I began to hate washing the dishes. I'd finish our pots and pans, get the dishwasher loaded and started, have a clean kitchen, and before you knew it there were more dirty dishes, spills, and stuff left out on the counter. A small and mundane thing, but nevertheless I was sick of doing it. Several things led to my dishwashing discontent: a need for control, some self-ishness, a bit of laziness, and simply being emotionally and physically drained by the demands of life. At some point it struck me that the only thing that could make this valuable, the only thing that could motivate me to do it without being miserable, was pretty simple. It was love. Washing the dishes was a way to love my wife and kids. Therefore, it was also a way to love God.

Benedictine nun and author Joan Chittister tells us that a secret to the spiritual life is "the significance of small things in a complex world. Small actions in social life, small efforts in the spiritual life, small moments in the personal life."[6] As Chittister points out, we live in a culture of excess that teaches us bigger is better. In such a culture, it really doesn't matter whether or not I do the dishes. Important people don't do the dishes; they've got more money to make, more power to gain, more fame to seek. In such a culture, not much that I do matters. Washing the dishes is a small thing. It doesn't matter. But I learned an important lesson. The small things matter. Here, as in everything, love makes all the difference. I learned that love gave meaning to washing the dishes. Love made it matter. It does the same for the rest of life.

Trying to write about the love of Christ is a bit over-whelming. There is so much to understand, say, and do in response to that love; whatever words we come up with seem inadequate. But that's to be expected. Love is the foundation of who Christ is. It is the foundation of the relationship between the members of the Trinity. It is foundational to the very nature and heart of God. Love should also be the foundation of who we are and how we live, as followers of the Way.

But we are often confused about the nature of love. One of my favorite short definitions of love is that it is "a well-reasoned devotion to the good or well-being of its objects."[7] God's love is *well-reasoned*. It is thoughtful, it is grounded in truth, and it includes a proper application of that truth to human life. God's love includes *devotion*. When we are devoted to something we give it our attention, our energy, in passionate and persistent ways. This is the kind of love God continually demonstrates for all of humanity, who bear his image. God's love for us is focused on our *well-being*, or *shalom*. God is devoted to us. He loves us in truth for our good. This leads us to another aspect of love that we shouldn't miss. Not only does it seek the good of others; love also seeks a deeper relationship, a deeper union, with them.

Such love is all over the narrative of the Bible. The love of God for Adam and Eve, for Israel, for the church, for the nations, and for the world is described on its pages. We are taught in Scripture that God is love (1 John 4:8), that Christ is the full representation to us of who God is (Col. 1:15, 19), and that we are to be imitators of Jesus (1 Cor. 11:1). But what is this love of God, exemplified in the character of Christ, that we are to imitate? There are many places to go if we want to understand this love, with an eye toward become more loving ourselves. But we can't go wrong reflecting on 1 Corinthians 13, which is perhaps the most well-known biblical description of the nature of love.

Most of us have probably heard this passage read at a wedding or two. While it is a beautiful picture of the kind of love a flourishing marriage exemplifies, that's not really what Paul has in mind here. Paul "did not write about *agapē* in order to rhapsodize about marriage; he was writing about the need for mutual concern and consideration *within the community of the church*."[8] We should do our best to understand the passage in light of that original purpose, even though it will have broader applications. With this in mind, then, let's look at the passage and reflect a bit on its significance for the Corinthian Christians, and for us:

> And I will show you a still more excellent way. If I speak in the tongues of mortals and of angels, but do not have love, I am a noisy gong or a clanging cymbal. And if I have prophetic powers, and understand all mysteries and all knowledge, and if I have all faith, so as to remove mountains, but do not have love, I am nothing. If I give away all my possessions, and if I hand over my body so that I may boast, but do not have love, I gain nothing.
>
> Love is patient; love is kind; love is not envious or boastful or arrogant or rude. It does not insist on its own way; it is not irritable or resentful; it does not rejoice in wrongdoing but rejoices in the truth. It bears all things, believes all things, hopes all things, endures all things.
>
> Love never ends. But as for prophecies, they will come to an end; as for tongues, they will cease; as for knowledge, it will come to an end. For we know

only in part, and we prophesy only in part; but when the complete comes, the partial will come to an end. When I was a child, I spoke like a child, I thought like a child, I reasoned like a child; when I became an adult, I put an end to childish ways. For now we see in a mirror, dimly, but then we will see face to face. Now I know only in part; then I will know fully, even as I have been fully known. And now faith, hope, and love abide, these three; and the greatest of these is love. (1 Cor. 12:31b–13:13)

We will look at this passage like we did Philippians 2:1–11, recognizing there is much more than we can cover here. But we'll dig in at some key points in ways that will help us not only understand love but become more loving people.

In order to understand this passage in the context of this epistle, we must keep the main idea of 1 Corinthians in mind.[9] This main idea is stated in 1:10: "Now I appeal to you, brothers and sisters, by the name of our Lord Jesus Christ, that all of you be in agreement and that there be no divisions among you, but that you be united in the same mind and the same purpose." This is the guiding idea of the letter. Paul is ultimately concerned that the Corinthians be united to one another and to Christ. They must eliminate division and cultivate unity of mind and purpose.

Our understanding and application of 1 Corinthians 13 must be guided by this main idea.[10] The passage beautifully exalts love, but as New Testament scholar Ben Witherington says, it is also "used in a deliberative argument to exhort the Corinthians to let love be their guiding principle in all that they say and do."[11] Another New Testament scholar, Craig Keener, echoes this when he says that Paul is not only exalting love but is also offering "an implicit reproof of his audience with the deliberate purpose of inviting them to change their behavior."[12]

Love is not just to be praised; it is to be practiced. It is the substance of "a still more excellent way." This more excellent way was the antidote to the divisions in the Corinthian church, as its members claimed they belonged to Paul, Apollos, Cephas, or Christ (1:12). Rather than uniting around a particular teacher or leader in opposition to others, they were to unite around Christ himself, who is love.

The relevance for Christians in America is clear. Love is the antidote to divisions in the church in America, just as it was for the church in Corinth. We claim allegiance to a particular pastor, influencer, or author. We may also give allegiance to a particular political party, perspective, or politician. Many of us then divide from those who do not share our allegiances. There may be times when this is justified, in extreme cases. But we treat too many cases as extreme. Rather than seeking the truth together, we verbally attack, ostracize, and even demonize our brothers and sisters in Christ who have different views. Paul's question to the Corinthians is apt for us as well: "Has Christ been divided?" (1 Cor. 1:13). Whether it is our favorite celebrity pastor, political party, or podcaster, we do not belong to them. We are people of the Way. Our ultimate allegiance is to Christ. This means our union with others who follow the Way must be counted as deeper and more significant than whatever disagreements we have about celebrity pastors or partisan politics. This is reasonable and good, because that union is grounded in Christ, not some celebrity.

Love is not just an abstract ideal. It is the essence of the Way. A follower of Jesus who does not seek to love God and others—including enemies, both real and imagined (Matt. 5:43–48)—is an oxymoron. We will struggle and fall short. But if, over the course of our lives, the love of God in Christ is not becoming more central to who we are and how we live, then something is deeply amiss. For this to happen, we need to know what love is. We need more than knowledge, but we do need knowledge.

Let's look at some key parts of 1 Corinthians 13, with an eye toward making the love of God in Christ more central to our lives. We've seen that this passage is written with the unity of the church in mind. We'll let this idea guide the rest of our exploration of love as it is described here.

Paul states that even if we speak in the tongues of humans and angels, even if we are gifted in prophecy, even if we have great understanding and knowledge, even if we have incredible mountain-moving faith, even if we give all that we have, including our very bodies—without love we are nothing and gain nothing (vv. 1–3). These are all good things, yet they are gutted of ultimate value if they are separated from love. When we selfishly seek power, spiritual gifts, or knowledge, we end up harming others and ourselves.

Examples of this abound. The past few years have seen numerous pastors and Christian leaders in America fall prey to ego and the lure of power, prestige, and wealth. Churches and ministries wrongly require non-disclosure agreements that have the effect of keeping abuse and other forms of sin in the dark, rather than bringing them into the light, which brings additional harms to those who have suffered. The details vary, but unrestrained ego and pride relentlessly lead to evil. Hurt and suffering abound. It might be sexual abuse; it might be protecting abusers rather than their victims; it might be serving money rather than God; it might be seeking recognition rather than the satisfaction of serving God in secret. It might be a million things, but one thing at the root of it all is pride. As Christ changes these deeper aspects of who we are, love and humility root out pride and enable us to serve God and others for their good, as well as our own.

The next section of our passage, vv. 4–7, has been seen by many as a description of the character of Christ, but it is also a description of the character his followers should seek to develop and of Paul's way of life as he imitates God. These four verses spell out in more detail what other-directed *agapē* love is like.

> Love *is* patient and kind.
> Love *is not* envious, boastful, arrogant, rude, irritable, or
>     resentful.
> Love *does not* insist on its own way or rejoice in
>     wrongdoing.
> Love *does* rejoice in the truth, and it bears, believes,
>     hopes, and endures all things.

Specific examples of the things that love *is not*, and that it *does not* rejoice in, can be found in other parts of 1 Corinthians. For example, Paul writes here that love is not envious, while earlier in 3:3 he rebukes the Corinthians for their envy.[13] Love is the antidote to many of the sins listed here, the very sins and struggles occurring in the Corinthian church.

Love is diametrically opposed to a way of life in which we see honor, fame, and other forms of recognition as a zero-sum game that we must play. Rather than fighting for our share (or more) of such things, over time a follower of the Way gains more and more freedom from such oppression of the ego. Love is also diametrically opposed to a hurried or abrasive impatience with others and with ourselves. It is relentlessly kind, rather than rude. As such, it contradicts the growing, shameful rudeness in our interactions with each other, in real life and online. While rudeness and irritability become more normal and even accepted, love calls us to a different way of life in our homes, at work, in our communities, and on social media. Love is a way of life with God and others at the center, rather than our ego, our desires, or our cherished opinions.

I've had to learn this lesson the hard way on social media. As a philosopher, I at times find it hard not to have an opinion about everything, and I'm too often disposed to share it. Beginning in 2015, I spent more time than I should engaging people on social media about controversial issues. After what I now see as several missteps, and even sin, I've learned how to engage in what I hope is a more humble and loving manner. Rather than giving in to that first impulse of online self-defense, or of anger and pride, I've worked at engaging others online in ways that I think Jesus would. Recently, I've spent much less time on social media, as I've come to believe that this is the will of Jesus for me. I hesitate to say this (this is a book about humility, after all!), but recently more than one person has expressed appreciation for how I engage on social media now, saying that they see me as somewhat of a role model here. This didn't happen to me at all several years ago, but it does now, and I share it to encourage you that change is possible for us. I take this to be evidence of some hard-won growth in my life, in dependence on the Spirit. I sometimes still have defensive, angry, or self-righteous impulses related to what I see on social media. Sometimes I give in to them. But when these feelings arise, I try to intentionally set them aside and engage others in humble and loving ways. Sometimes I immediately delete my tweet or comment, sometimes I stop typing halfway through one and move on. Sometimes—and I'm working toward this becoming more of a norm for me—I don't engage at all. We all need to seek insight and integrity related to how we engage others online. Our heart and actions in this realm of modern life must be suffused with love. Nothing less is fitting for followers of the Way.

Love rejoices in the truth, even when it is hard to hear. It rejoices in the truth even when it humbles us, which the truth tends to do. Truth in this passage has a moral sense. It is not just a matter of correct belief but of righteousness.[14] Since love unites us to God, to what is true and good, it enables us to bear and endure all things. For love to believe and hope all things does not entail some sort of irrationality, foolishness, or vain hope. Rather, as the New English Bible translates it, the point is that "there is no limit to its faith, its hope, and its endurance."[15] Love strengthens our character at its core. Love is wise, and it is strong.

The last section of our passage (vv. 8–13) contrasts love with the lesser goods of prophecy, knowledge, faith, and hope. These things have great value, but even that great value pales in comparison to the enduring great value of love. One reason for this is that while these other things will in some sense end, love never ends. It is a bridge between this age and the age to come. As Richard Hays observes, "love is the foretaste of our ultimate union with God, graciously given to us now and shared with our brothers and sisters. . . . [I]t will endure eternally when the love of God is all in all. . . . [I]t undergirds everything else and gives meaning to an otherwise unintelligible world."[16] Once we see God and ourselves more clearly, once we no longer see dimly but face-to-face, our faith and hope will be fulfilled. Our lives will finally be centered on love. It will be the substance of our very existence, forever.

What are loving people like, who seek to follow Christ in his love? They have a well-reasoned devotion to the well-being of those whom they love. They seek to center their lives on the God who is love. They fight against the forces of ego and pride, exemplifying instead a sacrificial devotion to the good of others. And they do so in ways that foster deeper relationships with God and their neighbors.

Love is not really that difficult to understand. Nothing in this passage is amorphous, overly abstract, or mysterious. The account of love it gives is pretty straightforward. The difficulty lies in becoming the kind of person who consistently demonstrates love. Paul's exhortation in 1 Corinthians 16:14—"Let all that you do be done in love"—is challenging and all-encompassing. But making progress in the practice of love, embracing and moving through the difficulties we'll encounter along the way, is worth it. When we do so, we experience a deeper union with God, reflect Christ to the world, work for the good of others, and enjoy the well-being of shalom for ourselves.

## Conclusion

Jesus Christ is *the* exemplar of both humility and love. These aren't just traits he has; they are part of the fabric of who he is. The humility and love demonstrated in his incarnation and crucifixion are remarkable. All things have been created through him and for him, and he holds all of creation together (Col. 1:16–17). Yet he still cares for us and prays for us, bringing requests on our behalf before the Father (Heb. 7:25). The Son of God praying to the Father for us—that reveals both his humility and his love.

Humility and love are vital for us as we seek union with Christ. These virtues orient us toward God and other people, and they include the desire to honor God and serve both him and our fellow human beings in sacrificial ways. These virtues are central to who Jesus is and to the very heart of the Trinity. They should also be central to us as we seek to follow him.

In the rest of this book we will rediscover the Way of Jesus, the Way of humility and love. We'll do this not only by rediscovering the role these virtues play in helping us develop good character and experience a deeper union with God, but also by exploring how to develop them in dependence on and in partnership with God and his church. We'll then be able to better exemplify humble love in our everyday lives.

## three

# A People of the Way

Imagine you're living a simple, quiet life. I know, this is hard to imagine with all the noise, chaos, controversy, and hurried pace of our lives. But go ahead and try it. Imagine you live in a small, picturesque mountain village, caring for and loving your children along with your spouse. Your days are filled with hard, exhausting, but satisfying work. There are also moments of rest and play, moments of goodness and beauty with your family, in the world God created. You relish these moments. God, your family, your work, your church, your community, and God's creation all bring you joy. But you're also starting to sense something. It's something you don't want to see but can't ignore or avoid. Something evil—truly, horribly, undeniably evil—is starting to grow in your country. In your village. You realize that you may be a part of that evil. And you realize that opposing it may cost you everything, including your life.

This is the story of Austrian farmer and Christian martyr Franz Jägerstätter. His story is beautifully and hauntingly told in the film *A Hidden Life*.[1] When the Nazis came into Austria, Jägerstätter was the only person in his village to vote against the unification of Austria and Germany. He also took a public stand by refusing to fight for the Nazis. Sadly, he stood alone. When Jägerstätter was called up for military duty in 1943, he refused to fight for Hitler. As he left his village early one morning to face the consequences of his stand, Jägerstätter ran into a childhood friend. In reply to his friend's greeting, he said, "You'll see no more of me."[2] He was right. Jägerstätter was jailed for his refusal to fight. On August 9, 1943, he was beheaded by the Nazis. He left behind his wife of seven years and their three daughters. The oldest was five.

Why? Why would he do this? As one biographer puts it, when Jägerstätter was given orders "to serve in a war he considered unjust—a war, moreover, which he felt would serve the evil purposes of an intrinsically immoral political regime—[he] refused to comply, and in his refusal accepted the death he knew would follow."[3] His Christian conscience and his Christlike character made being complicit with this evil impossible for him.

In the past two millennia, many have died because of their resolute commitment to Christ. Some of these martyrs are famous. We know their stories. Most remain anonymous, for now. We, too, are called to give our lives to Christ and his kingdom. While for many Christians around the world martyrdom is a real possibility, the chances of this are very low in my country, the United States. But no matter what, there remains a cost of discipleship for everyone who follows Jesus. Sometimes that cost can be steep. But along with the cost are the many blessings, the many good things, of life in Christ. There is, as has been said, a cost of non-discipleship, too. We lose out on so much if we refuse to allow Christ access to all of our lives.

In the Gospel of Mark, Peter wrestles with these issues, and Jesus reminds him of the costs and the blessings of following him:

> Peter began to say to him, "Look, we have left everything and followed you." Jesus said, "Truly I tell you, there is no one who has left house or brothers or sisters or mother or father or children or fields, for my sake and for the sake of the good news, who will not receive a hundredfold now in this age—houses, brothers and sisters, mothers and children, and fields, with persecutions—and in the age to come eternal life. But many who are first will be last, and the last will be first." (Mark 10:28–31)

Some end up sacrificing more than the things listed here by Jesus. Some, like Franz Jägerstätter, give their lives. Yet even that ultimate sacrifice is overcome by Jesus on our behalf. He who is the resurrection and the life gives us eternal life.

While most of us will not end up dying for our faith, there is something that we are all called to do, something we share as Christians. We are called to be followers of the Way *in this world* (Acts 24:14), the very same Way that led Jägerstätter to his death. It took great humility, and great love, to be able to make this sacrifice. Jägerstätter was a person of the Way. We can be, too.

## The Foundation and the Roof

One reason the story of Franz Jägerstätter touches us so deeply is that it is a beautiful picture of both humility and love. Humility and love were essential parts of his character. He could not have made the choices he did without these virtues. Humility and love are essential for us, too, if we are seeking to be more like Christ, to become "little Christs." One reason for this is that they help us grow in other virtues. Vincent de Paul describes their importance for Christian character as follows: "Humility and charity [i.e., love] are the two master chords: one, the lowest; the other, the highest; all the others are dependent on them. Therefore, it is necessary, above all, to maintain ourselves in these two virtues; for observe well that the preservation of the whole edifice depends on the foundation and the roof."[4] We would do well to heed this advice. If we prioritize growth in humility and in love, in the context of our union with Christ and his church, many good things will follow. We'll grow in other virtues, more fully love God and our neighbors, and more fully receive God's love, too.

Many Christians, past and present, have extolled the virtues of humility and love. Humility is foundational. It's the root of a developed, and a developing, Christian character. We've already seen that Christ is the paradigm of true humility. That is reason enough for us to pursue it. Many have praised this virtue, and we should heed their unified voice. Gregory the Great states that "humility is the guardian of virtue."[5] Similarly, Bonaventure contends that humility is "the root and guardian of all virtues."[6] Dietrich von Hildebrand tells us that humility is "the fountainhead of all specifically human virtues."[7] John Cassian believed that the very structure of virtue in the human soul is built on "the foundations of true humility."[8] Teresa of Ávila taught that "so long as we are on this earth, nothing matters more to us than humility."[9] Benedict gave those in his monastery twelve practical steps for cultivating humility, as he knew this virtue was crucial for life in a flourishing monastic community.[10] This is true for any flourishing Christian community, not just a monastic one. Humility leads to a spiritually healthy community; pride is a destructive force in any community. John Climacus also praises humility, observing that "the sun lights up everything visible. Likewise, humility is the source of everything done according to reason. Where there is no light, all is darkness. Where there is no humility, all is rotten."[11] Finally, Andrew Murray writes that humility is "the one indispensable condition for fellowship with Jesus."[12] One biblical reason for all of this is that "God opposes the proud, but gives grace to the humble" (James 4:6). Humility opens us up to the grace of God and is itself a product of that grace. The other-centeredness of humility grounds the other virtues, enabling us to put the interests of others ahead of our own. This creates a foundation for virtues like forgiveness, compassion, and generosity, to name just a few.

Love is also crucial for followers of Jesus. It is vital for a developed, and a developing, Christian character. We've already looked at Paul's teaching about love in 1 Corinthians 13. In Colossians 3, Paul instructs Christians to clothe ourselves with love, and he teaches that love binds everything together in perfect unity. Here, "everything" refers to the virtues of compassion, kindness, meekness, humility, patience, and forgiveness. The First Letter of John 4:16 famously says that "God is love" and that "those who abide in love abide in God, and God abides in them."

Many others have extolled this virtue, and we should heed their voices. Teresa of Ávila exhorts her sisters concerning the centrality of love, saying, "the Lord does not look so much at the magnitude of anything we do as at the love with which we do it."[13] Our motives matter, and love is an essential motive for followers of Christ. Thomas Merton says, "the things that we love tell us what we are."[14] What we love reveals our true character. Augustine exhorts us to have rightly ordered loves. The just and holy person "forms an unprejudiced estimate of things, and keeps his affections also under strict control, so that he neither loves what he ought not to love, nor fails to love what he ought to love, nor loves that more which ought to be loved less.... [B]ut God is to be loved for His own sake ... all things are to be loved in reference to God."[15] If we love God first, all of our other loves will tend to fall into their proper place. We will make progress in loving what we should love, in the right way, and to the right degree. One result of this is that we will act in loving ways. As bell hooks puts it, "Love is as love does."[16]

The other virtues are dependent on humility and love. How so? First, they are built upon the foundation of humility. The foundation is essential to the structural integrity of a home. A faulty foundation ultimately leads to a collapse. Humility plays such a role in our lives. As we humble ourselves and draw near to God, God draws near to us. Humility is both a product and a means of divine grace. The other-centeredness of humility makes it possible for us to grow in the other virtues, as they depend on this other-centeredness as a foundation for their existence and growth. For example, compassion requires that we focus on the suffering of others and what we can do to help alleviate it. Second, as the roof, love covers the other virtues. A roof protects a home from the onslaught of the elements, keeping it safe from the wind, rain, snow, and sun. Love protects us from the onslaught of the unholy trinity of the world, the flesh, and the devil. Love gives other virtues the opportunity to grow in us, enabling us to mature in Christ as we seek to love God, our neighbor, and ourselves.

Humility and love are mutually reinforcing virtues. Growth in one of them often entails growth in the other. Augustine, for example, believed that love is perfected in humility.[17] These virtues also require each other. As Teresa of Ávila puts it, "I cannot understand how humility exists, or can exist, without love, or love without humility."[18] Why is this? Both humility and love emphasize self-denial for the good of others, valuing others above oneself. Both can require great sacrifice. In this chapter we'll explore their connections with several other virtues, including faith, wisdom, compassion, justice, self-control, forgiveness, and courage. We'll look at how they undermine the vices of pride and sloth, traits that can poison one's character and one's community. Again, it is vital that we remember this is all done in the context of the pursuit of a deeper union with God, fueled by his grace. This is not a moral self-help program with a Christian veneer. It's not a spiritually foolish exercise in self-righteousness. It's not even a quest for personal happiness, ultimately. It is entering as fully as we can into a transformational union with God in Christ, where we are becoming, in the fullest sense of the term, *saved*.

## Humility and Character

We recently bought an older home. It was built in the 1920s, and we knew going in that it needed a lot of work. Nearly all the plumbing and electrical systems needed to be updated, there were some serious drainage issues in the backyard, and the kitchen was in bad shape. We had the home thoroughly inspected prior to closing, and while the list of needed work was long, we were relieved that there were no issues with the foundation of the house. It was in good shape. In order for a home to be sturdy, a strong foundation is essential. If the foundation is faulty, the whole structure could collapse.

Christ is the ultimate foundation of our lives (1 Cor. 3:11). Humility connects us in unique ways to Jesus, our foundation and cornerstone. To build and maintain a sturdy and solid Christlike character, humility is essential. It is foundational to our character. What is the truly humble person like? As we have seen, such a person, following the pattern of Jesus, fights to descend the social ladder rather than climb it. He makes the interests of others his priority, rather than his own. This is central to the virtue of humility. Instead of always grasping for what he wants, the humble person serves others, for their good, often in sacrificial ways. The humble person focuses on God and others, rather than himself. The humble person is steeped in the love of God, and that love flows from God through him to others. This kind of humility is connected not only to love but also to other virtues, to our character, in many ways. As we look at several other Christian virtues, we'll start to see connections with humility. We'll be more motivated to cultivate humility, by God's grace. And we'll be on our way to experiencing the kind of transformation in Christ that humility is conducive to, paving the way for other Christian virtues—faith, wisdom, compassion, justice, self-control, forgiveness, and courage—as well as a deeper union with God.

Faith is not mere belief; it is something more like trust. I like the way Paul Moser puts it, when he says that faith involves "entrusting oneself to God."[19] This way of capturing what faith is helps us see that it includes trusting Christ not only for the forgiveness of our sins but for so much more—for everything, in fact. In faith we entrust our selves, our very lives, to God. Such faith includes allegiance to God. In fact, one could go so far as to claim that faith in Jesus also means allegiance to him as our king.[20] This allegiance includes belief that the gospel is true, a profession of loyalty to Jesus as our king, and embodied faithfulness to him as our true king. If I really am entrusting myself to Christ, I will have a growing allegiance to him in my heart, mind, words, and deeds. As we grow in faith, we spend less energy on managing our lives for the sake of comfort, power, pleasure, wealth, or whatever it is that we sometimes desire more than Christ and his kingdom. This freedom from managing my life is a freedom that I long to experience in more wide-ranging and deeper ways. I've made some progress, but I want so much more. I'm sure you do as well. Yet it is so easy to try to exercise control over our lives, other people, and our circumstances, often in very subtle ways. And this is where humility comes into play. We can't control our lives in these ways; doing so is beyond our capabilities. In humility, we see not only that we can't do this, but also that we shouldn't.

During graduate school, a psychologist helped me to see what was a revelation for me at the time. I was trying to control things I simply couldn't control as a response to feeling like everything was out of my control. As I worked on my dissertation I wondered if I'd ever get a job as a philosophy professor. So much of my future was unclear. Seeking to control the outcomes of my choices in graduate school and in other parts of my life was simply me trying to be God. This is a role we are obviously unsuited for. Humility puts our human limits into sharp relief. It shows us that we are not suitable objects of allegiance and that Jesus is. The humble person is able to have an allegiance to something greater than herself, to someone greater than herself. Humility clears the way for a deeper faith in God, and it continues to nourish such faith as we abide in Christ.

One definition of wisdom is the "ability to make right decisions."[21] Wisdom is a practical virtue. The wise person makes good, prudent, and helpful decisions that are in accord with reality. She understands what is true and is able to apply it to her life with excellence.

Humility and wisdom are also deeply connected virtues. Proverbs 11:2 says that "wisdom is with the humble." The humble person is wise because she acknowledges and lives in light of her limits and puts the interests of others ahead of her own. But such a person is also wise because in humility she is better able to see things as they are, to make her way through life according to reality. Pride produces distortions in our hearts and minds. The humble person, in wisdom, avoids them. What sort of distortions? They are legion. Consider the fact that most of us engage in self-serving bias. We think that we are better than most other people across many domains of life.[22] We tend to take credit for our successes but make excuses for or pass the buck on our failures. For example, studies show that when students do well on a test, they believe it is because of their ability and the work they did to prepare for it. But when they do poorly, they are more likely to think there was some sort of problem with the way the exam was set up. Teachers do the same sort of thing. When their students succeed, teachers take credit. When a student fails, it is somehow the student's—not the teacher's—fault. We tend to think we are better than others in so many other ways. We think we are more ethical, intelligent, and capable at our jobs, to name a few examples. Of course, it is not possible for most of us to be above average. But we think we are. In humility, the wise person adopts an unbiased perspective.[23] Wisdom and humility, working together, can weaken our tendencies toward self-serving bias.

But such wisdom is not easy. Consider something called the Dunning-Kruger effect. This is a tendency some people have to believe that they have more knowledge than they in fact do. They are not aware of their lack of knowledge. Such people don't know enough to know that they don't know what they think they know! (You may need to read that again.) The point is that such people overestimate their knowledge. While this may be humorous in trivial things, when important goods are on the line it can be deadly. This effect, and other manifestations of our foolish and prideful self-serving bias, can damage us, our relationships, and our communities in many ways. Humility undercuts this. It helps us to see the truth about ourselves and the world and then wisely order our lives according to the truth.

Humility also fosters growth in the virtue of compassion. The compassionate person believes that the suffering of others matters. He has a desire to enter into that suffering, to share it, and to alleviate it. Compassion leads us to act. Joseph Butler, an eighteenth-century British pastor, theologian, and philosopher, says that in our relationships with others, when we "compassionate their distresses, we, as it were, substitute them for ourselves, their interest for our own; and have the same kind of . . . sorrow in their distress, as we have . . . upon our own."[24] I love that the term "compassionate" is used as a verb here. We are to compassion*ate* the suffering of others. We certainly see this in the life of Christ. His compassion was not merely a belief or emotion; it also led him to act. The same should be true of us.

Humility can help us grow in compassion in various ways, but I'd like to share one that resonates with my own experience. In many ways, I'm a pretty nonjudgmental person (not all, but many). I'm fairly good at giving grace to others, much better than I am at receiving it myself. But like most of us, I know that certain things can set me off, at least internally. Becoming more aware of my own particular weaknesses and the depths of my own sin has actually helped me to grow in compassion for others. Many in the history of the church have recognized that humility involves having a low view of ourselves, but in a particular sense. It is not the case that we are worthless, useless, or have no value, though many think of humility this way. Rather, we have value as creatures who bear God's image, who are loved and valued by God. Yet humility reminds us that we are fallen human beings, creatures who struggle with sin. We are morally and spiritually broken. We can be frail. In fact, many have testified that as they've experienced growth in Christ, they've also become more aware of their own sinfulness and frailty. Humility, then, is a way of knowing ourselves more deeply.

As I become aware of my sin and frailty and in humility realize how some struggles persist in my life, I can also see that others are in the same boat. Their struggles might be different from mine, but we share a common weakness that manifests itself in different ways. In my own life, impatience and defensiveness can still rear their ugly heads, even as I think I've made progress. The realization that others have the same experience, but with different vices and struggles, helps me to have compassion for them. Often, people are not being willfully prideful, self-centered, or controlling, any more than I am being willfully prideful, defensive, or impatient. It just comes out of them, for a variety of reasons. The same is true for me. This enables me to be more compassionate with others, to suffer with them, because I truly can identify with their experience. We're all struggling. Personal history, personality, character, environment, and many other things come together and yield both good and bad fruit in our lives. Their bad fruit might be different from mine, but at a deeper level we have the same struggle. Seeing others and ourselves in this way gives great opportunities for showing others, and ourselves, the compassion we all need. It can help us compassionate the suffering of others, as Butler would say.

Finally, consider the connections between humility and justice. There are many different ways to understand justice, in our personal and social lives. When we hear the word "justice," we tend to think about civil and criminal law and our criminal justice system. These days many also think about the controversies surrounding different views about social justice. Our focus is different here. We'll zero in on justice as a personal virtue, though this has implications not only for our relationships with others but also for the institutions and systems in our society, including the criminal justice system. Personal justice and social justice are connected.

How are we to understand the virtue of justice? A person who has the virtue of justice tends to give people what they are due.[25] This tells us something about justice, but not enough. What do we owe to other people? What are they, in fact, due? This can be difficult to answer, and some of our modern sensibilities about justice can lead us astray. Depending on our beliefs, some of us may tend to one extreme or the other. Some think we don't owe others much, if anything, at least not those outside of our immediate circle of family and friends. Others might take on too much under the obligations of justice.

The answer has to do with *the goal* of the virtue of justice, which is that people would be in right relationships with one another. The result of this is peace and harmony in those relationships. So much is set against justice in our world, including some churches and Christian institutions: protecting abusive leaders and further harming their victims; ignoring the dignity of those with disabilities; putting the Second Amendment ahead of the Sermon on the Mount; demonizing immigrants rather than demonstrating the love of Christ toward them; protecting our wealth and power, rather than putting them to work for others; serving mammon rather than our Maker; denigrating human life in so many ways, across the spectrum of life, rather than honoring its dignity.

As with many virtues, the context will be important as we seek to be just. General principles help, but we also need wisdom to determine the relevance of justice for any particular situation. A right relationship with my spouse, close friend, child, coworker, acquaintance, immigrant, or person on the other side of the planet will look different in every case. The Golden Rule is clearly relevant, as is the Great Commandment. We are to do to others as we would have them do to us (Matt. 7:12). We are to love God with all we are and our neighbors as ourselves (Matt. 22:37–39). In seeking to be just, we might ask ourselves what we would want if we were in others' shoes. In the shoes of a spouse or good friend, we might want more time or less selfishness. For an immigrant, we would want more humane policies and the chance to work. For a person on the other side of the planet, perhaps less conspicuous consumption or a donation to a reputable charity that meets important needs is what is required. The just person, then, is someone who flourishes in part because she contributes to the common good, helping others in her community and even around the world flourish, too. Since we are social creatures, in need of each other, being rightly related to each other helps all of us to flourish. The just person habitually acts in ways that nourish her relationships with others, contributing to her own good and to the common good.

Humility is important to our perception and practice of justice. It includes an awareness of our limits and of our dependence on others. This helps us to reject the myth that people get what they deserve (the rich, healthy, powerful, and happy deserve what they have, as do the poor, sick, marginalized, and unhappy). We realize that so much of our welfare, health, and happiness depends on others. Reflecting on this can turn our minds to the injustices that others face. Or it might help us see the injustices we face and motivate us to band together with others to change things. We can't fix or work on everything, but we can do our part in our homes, neighborhoods, churches, town or city, and, to some extent, nation and world. I suspect for most of us, the majority of our focus will tend to be more local, but it depends on our individual callings and capabilities.

Humility also undermines sin, in particular the vices that are at the root of so much evil in us and our world.

We'll focus on pride. The proud person is arrogant, ego-tistical, and self-centered.[26] C. S. Lewis calls pride both "the great sin" and "the utmost evil."[27] He observes that pride leads to all of the other vices and that "it is the complete anti-God state of mind."[28] He describes it as the cancer of the spiritual life. Lewis is not alone here. In the history of Christian thought, pride is seen by many to be the root of all sin and vice. It is the root of the seven deadly sins: vainglory, envy, sloth, greed, anger, gluttony, and lust. Given this, the more we can remove pride from our lives, the more we are able to remove these seven deadly vices that wreak so much havoc in our lives and world. Humility, by undermining pride, cuts the seven deadly sins off from what feeds them, which in turn brings life to us and others.

Pride comes in a variety of forms.[29] One form is intellectual pride. The intellectually proud person fails to appreciate the fact that his mind is both finite and fallible. Such pride makes us more susceptible to ideological and personal biases. In such pride we pretend that we have the complete, full, and final grasp of the truth. We are blind to our limits and to the ways our devotion to our self-interest clouds our thinking. Yet we also believe we see these limits and failings, quite clearly, in other people. Humility counteracts such pride. The humble are aware of their intellectual limitations, both those of human beings in general and their own particular ones. The other-centeredness of humility, the disposition to put the interests of others ahead of our own (Phil. 2:1–11), works against our devotion to our self-interest, which helps remove its influence from our thinking.

Another form of pride is moral pride. This kind of pride is manifested when we condemn others for failing to live up to our moral standards. We act as if our standards are God's standards, but we fail to see that often they are not. One example I run into fairly often where I live is the debate about whether Christians should drink alcohol.[30] Many claim that doing so is strictly forbidden by God, that abstinence from alcohol is the only option for followers of Jesus. Some point to Ephesians 5:18, which says "Do not get drunk with wine, for that is debauchery; but be filled with the Spirit." Others refer to the wisdom from the book of Proverbs, such as 20:1, "Wine is a mocker, strong drink a brawler, and whoever is led astray by it is not wise" (see also Prov. 23:20, 29–31). Alcohol is implicated in a lot of social and relational problems, including drunk driving, many forms of assault and abuse, as well as a significant portion of criminal acts. It causes significant pain and suffering in marriages, families, and friendships. It clearly has the power to do great harm and undermine our flourishing.

Others disagree with an absolute prohibition for all, pointing out the ways in which the Bible talks about wine and other alcoholic beverages as a blessing (Deut. 14:22–26; Ps. 104:15). In *The Spirituality of Wine*, Gisela Kreglinger discusses how wine in particular is seen throughout the Bible as a gift and blessing from God, given to us for our enjoyment.[31] She points out that wine is included in Isaac's blessing of Jacob (Gen. 27:28), brings cheer to human beings (Judg. 9:13), and is a sign of God's redemption (Joel 2:19–24; Zech. 8:12). She observes that "Jesus himself seems to have enjoyed wine regularly. He must have done so often enough that his fellow Hebrews became uneasy with it. They accused him of being a drunkard."[32] Of course, it was a false accusation. In the future, Jesus once again will drink of the fruit of the vine with his followers, in the kingdom of his Father (Matt. 26:29). Wine is seen as a good thing in Scripture—a gift and blessing from God, a part of our eternal life together with God when all is set right and his kingdom comes in its fullness.

I think alcohol can be a good thing received with gratitude from the hand of God. Obviously this doesn't mean that getting drunk is okay. But it does mean that in moderation, there are ways to enjoy alcohol that are virtuous. Ultimately, as in all things, love is the most important consideration here. Love for God, others, and ourselves is central. Alcohol can be abused, misused, and valued too highly. Alcohol should not be used as a substitute to dull the pain that we ought to be taking to God and to those in our community of faith. Like many other good things, we may choose to abstain from it for the sake of our relationship with God or our love for others. But we may also choose to enjoy it if we are able to do so in ways that are honoring to God and loving toward ourselves and others. And we should, in humility, agree to disagree with others who don't share our convictions here, rather than condemning them. We don't all have to agree on everything. We should be mindful of the fact that on many issues there is room for faithful followers of the Way to disagree. Humility enables us to do so. Love binds us together in the midst of such disagreements.

Lastly, let's consider how humility counteracts spiritual pride, which is an offshoot of moral pride. Spiritual pride happens when I claim that God sanctions my beliefs and convictions, in particular my moral and theological beliefs (these days we should add political views, sadly). In spiritual pride, I believe that God is my exclusive ally. He's for *me*, and against *them*. I'm on the side of good; they are on the side of evil.

Think of the person who identifies *their interpretation of Scripture* on some issue with *the teachings of Scripture itself*, when people of sound mind and good heart, committed to the Way, disagree. It is good to remember that on theological issues that fall outside of mere Christianity, humility counsels us to avoid exalting our interpretation on issues where there is room for disagreement. Spiritual pride shows up in our politics these days. One Republican congressman recently shared voicemail messages he's received, messages monitored by interns at his office in DC. One person left the following: "Wrath of the Lord God Almighty come upon you, your health, your family, your home, your livelihood. And I'll pray if it be God's will that you suffer."[33] Spiritual pride, indeed. I've been told numerous times that to be a faithful Christian in the United States one must be a Republican. To be a Democrat, they claim, is to oppose God. But no political party, right, left, or center, accurately embodies all the values of God's kingdom or consistently does so better than the others. These are flawed human institutions. Thankfully our ultimate loyalty does not belong to a political party, nor to our country, but rather to Christ and his kingdom. Humility reminds us all of these truths. And love urges us to transcend the polarization of partisan politics and the self-righteousness of theological superiority.

Many people make use of Christianity as a means to power, wealth, and self-exaltation. They use the Way as a means of getting their own way. But the humble person will refuse to do this, just as Jesus refused to do in his incarnation, life, and death on a cross. The humble person is not concerned with her place in some hierarchy. Instead, she focuses on working with God for the good of others. In this way, she is allied with God, but she doesn't see God as her exclusive ally. In fact, she sees all people as allies of God, at least potentially so, as they all bear the divine image. In that spirit, she humbly serves.

Given the ways humility nourishes, fosters, and strengthens many virtues, and how it undermines the powerful vice of pride, growth in humility tends to foster growth in our overall character. Growth in humility fosters a wider and deeper growth in Christ. It is the foundation of a growing and healthy character, in a growing and healthy relationship with Christ and his body, the church.

## Love and Character

That old house we bought needed a lot of work, inside and out. But one of the very first things we had to do was replace the leaky roof. To ignore that while making structural and cosmetic changes inside the house would leave all of that expensive and time-consuming work vulnerable to one strong rainstorm. My wife has a knack for creating beauty in and around our home, but it would be foolish to do so and leave it unprotected from the elements. Once we had a new roof, we were able to get to work on the rest of the house. Obviously a good roof is needed to preserve and protect the home. Without it, not only will the home itself be vulnerable but the foundation will ultimately weaken, too. The roof protects the foundation by keeping water away from it. It is essential.

To maintain a sturdy Christlike character, we need the virtue of love. As we have seen, love is like a roof. It is essential. Those who have the virtue of love have a well-reasoned devotion to the good of others. They seek to center their lives on the God who is love. They are committed to a sacrificial devotion to the good of others. They do all of this in ways that foster deeper relationships with God and their neighbor. Love preserves and protects these relationships. It does the same for our character. It provides an environment where we can flourish, where we can become and be people of good character, moving toward becoming little Christs.

Love is connected to other virtues, to our overall character, in many ways. We'll look at how love is connected to self-control, forgiveness, and courage. As we apply what we learn, we'll be on our way to experiencing the kind of transformation in Christ that love produces, paving the way for other Christian virtues and a deeper union with God.

Self-control is a fruit of the Holy Spirit in the life of the Christian (Gal. 5:22–23). It is a natural result of the Spirit-filled life, a daily yielding to and dependence upon the Holy Spirit. At first glance, love and self-control might not seem like a natural pairing of virtues. How does love, understood as a well-reasoned devotion to the good of others (and ourselves), help us grow in the virtue of self-control? Proverbs 25:28 tells us, "Like a city breached, without walls, is one who lacks self-control." Failures of self-control can have negative consequences in our lives. A lack of it may cost us money, waste our time, have a negative impact on our physical or psychological health, or have harmful consequences in our relationships with God and others.

What is self-control? Thomas Aquinas takes self-control, or temperance, to be the virtue that directs our desires for physical pleasures so that they support what our reason judges to be good.[34] The person with self-control is not at the mercy of his desire for some pleasure, but rather is able to exercise discipline in his pursuit of what is good and holy. The person with the virtue of self-control is able to control his desires and say no to them when they conflict with what his God-given reason tells him is good.

Self-control is related to love of the self. How we treat our bodies and respond to our bodily desires is an area of life where self-control and love work in tandem. Our bodies are holy. They are temples of God (1 Cor. 6:19). As such, self-control is vital to how we treat them and what we do with them. We are to avoid sexual immorality, gluttony, and a host of other sins and vices that undermine our physical and psychological flourishing.

For many of us, the first things that may come to mind when thinking about self-control are finances, diet, or exercise. No doubt these are important areas for exercising self-control. Our love for others, those close to us as well as anyone else in need, can be expressed by how generous we are with our money. Through physical exercise and a proper diet we treat our body as the temple it is. Self-control in relation to the body is an important way to love oneself.

But other dimensions of our lives are relevant, too. We can broaden the scope of self-control to include more than just the pleasures of the body. Think of the pleasure, albeit short-lived, of expressing unrighteous anger in our speech, of verbally denigrating another person, or of sharing a choice bit of gossip. It can be hard to exercise self-control in the words we use with and about others:

> The tongue is placed among our members as a world of iniquity; it stains the whole body, sets on fire the cycle of nature, and is itself set on fire by hell. For every species of beast and bird, of reptile and sea creature, can be tamed and has been tamed by the human species, but no one can tame the tongue—a restless evil, full of deadly poison. With it we bless the Lord and Father, and with it we curse people, made in the likeness of God. From the same mouth comes a blessing and a curse. My brothers and sisters, this ought not to be so. ( James 3:6–10 )

We can now see more clearly another way self-control is related to love. When I truly love another person—a family member, friend, or enemy—I will not curse them. I will not denigrate or disparage them. Instead, I will see and speak about them as they are, human beings made in the image of God. Fallen human beings, like me, but nevertheless human beings of great dignity and intrinsic worth, who should be blessed rather than cursed. This doesn't mean my words must always be *nice*, but they must be *loving*. For example, those who are oppressed, marginalized, or persecuted may speak the truth about injustice to their oppressors, in clear and forceful ways that are nevertheless still loving.

In the long run, as we are renewed in Christ, the struggle to exercise self-control in this and other areas of life will decrease. We will have the habit of living as Christ would if he were us, of being like him, in more and more areas of our lives, as the Spirit works in us and we grow in dependence upon that gracious power. We will be like a spring, pouring forth speech that is like fresh water, because our hearts have been transformed: "The good person out of the good treasure of the heart produces good, and the evil person out of evil treasure produces evil, for it is out of the abundance of the heart that the mouth speaks" (Luke 6:45). As this transformation of the heart takes hold, we'll naturally speak words of blessing, in love, to and about others: family, friends, and even our enemies.

Forgiving others, like self-control, can be difficult. So is being the type of person who is disposed to forgive, someone who has the virtue of forgiveness. Perhaps this is one reason why these words are included in the Lord's Prayer: "And forgive us our debts, as we also have forgiven our debtors" (Matt. 6:12). Our experience of forgiveness in Christ should make us more forgiving people. As we experience the forgiving love of Jesus, we ought to become the kind of people who extend that same forgiving love to others.

Forgiveness is a great good; granting and receiving it are good for us. In love, in a well-reasoned devotion to the good of another, by granting forgiveness we make possible the goods of reconciliation in the relationship, as well as removing the evils of bitterness, resentment, and even hatred from both the forgiven and the forgiver. Love can move us to forgive others, as we truly desire what is good for them. Love plays a part in releasing them from the guilt they are experiencing as a result of what they have done or failed to do. This is not the forgiveness of cheap grace, however. A deep repentance on the part of the offender is vital.

Experiencing forgiveness is also connected to love. It can lead to a deeper ability to love others. In Luke 7:36–50, Jesus is dining at the home of a Pharisee. A woman who has heard he is there comes to see him, bringing a jar of alabaster ointment. She weeps, wiping her tears from the feet of Jesus with her hair and anointing them with the ointment. The Pharisee is not impressed, thinking to himself that if Jesus were really a prophet he would know that this woman is "a sinner" and wouldn't allow her to do these things. But Jesus praises her as an exemplar not only of hospitality but also of someone whose experience of forgiveness leads her to love: "her sins, which were many, have been forgiven; hence she has shown great love" (Luke 7:47). There is something about receiving forgiveness for our many sins that can lead us to show great love. At least part of this arises from our gratitude for that forgiveness. But in this case, I suspect that this great love was also a result of her experience of God's forgiveness, grace, mercy, and love. The deeply offensive

nature of sin, nullified by the more deeply powerful nature of God's merciful, gracious, and loving forgiveness,
is followed by great love in the life of the one who has
been forgiven.

If we are struggling to love others, especially those
who have sinned against us, this is understandable. One
way to help us forgive, when it is called for, is to reflect
on our own experience of God's gracious forgiveness
and let that fuel our love for others. Love brings forth
forgiveness, and forgiveness produces love, in a truly
virtuous cycle. But the process may take time, and we
should be honest with God about the difficulties as we
walk through this with him.

In his study of forgiveness, R. Douglas Geivett observes that there has been a growing focus on the personal benefits of forgiveness, emphasizing a therapeutic
understanding of the value of being a forgiving person.[35]
It is often true that we will feel better if we forgive others. We will experience emotional healing, be physically
and psychologically healthier, and replace anger and
bitterness with peace and freedom. These are all good
things, and it is significant that being a forgiving person
has such benefits. They are not, however, the primary
motivations for being a forgiving person as a follower of
the Way. As Geivett points out, the primary reason for
being a forgiving person has more to do with the health
of the body of Christ and our relationship with God than
with the personal therapeutic benefits. We forgive because Jesus does and expects us to do the same, as the
Lord's Prayer makes clear—"as we also have forgiven our
debtors." We forgive because this is how we protect and

promote unity and love in our Christian community. We forgive because it helps us be that shining city on a hill, giving others a picture of how the kingdom of God works, with an open invitation to enter that kingdom. Certainly we can be grateful for the personal benefits we experience as we forgive others. But if that is our only or even main concern, we are missing the boat. True forgiveness is not about me. It is about us. It is about love. Ultimately, it is about God.

Like forgiveness, a distinctly Christian picture of courage will challenge some of the ways our culture thinks of this virtue.[36] Many think of courage as the virtue exemplified by the soldier or action hero as he faces adversity and overcomes fear. This form of courage is shown when one risks his life in battle against the enemy to protect others and fights to stay alive himself. This heroic warrior kind of courage is grounded in strength, weapons, and human power. But there is another form of courage, one that draws upon the example of Christ and is deeply rooted in Christian thought.

The paradigm of courage in the Christian tradition is not the soldier; it is the martyr. It is not Captain America; it is Jesus Christ. The martyr, rather than confronting evil and adversity with human power or weapons, has been stripped of her ability to save her own life. Rather than the courage of aggression, she possesses the courage of endurance. The only way for the martyr to keep her life is by renouncing her faith. But she is not willing to do so. She resists. She is willing to suffer and die for Christ, just as Christ was willing to suffer and die for humanity. She is resolute, not allowing her fear of suffering or death to control her. Something else gives her soul the strength to courageously endure.

That something else is love. In fact, love plays a role in the courage of the warrior and of the martyr. Both share, as Rebecca Konyndyk DeYoung points out, "a willingness to risk death for the sake of something they love."[37] The warrior loves his fellow soldiers, his friends and family, and his country. This love can motivate him to stand and fight. The courage of the Ukrainian people in the face of the ongoing Russian invasion of their nation comes to mind. Love for God can motivate this kind of courage. Love also plays a central role in the courage of the martyr. The martyr is willing to suffer and possibly die because of her great love for God. To exemplify courage, at risk to one's own life, one must love something more than that life. This Christian ideal of courage is exemplified by Christ, who endured death for the sake of love, a love for God the Father and for all of humanity.

How is this form of courage, the courage of the martyr, relevant to Christians who will not face death for their faith? DeYoung writes that the *enduring nature* of such courage is the key, that "the main point of making martyrdom the paradigm of courage is to show that this virtue can find expression as much or more in suffering or weakness as it can in striking out against a threat."[38] It also "enables anyone willing to endure suffering for the sake of love to echo this supreme example of courage in their own lives, and leaves physical power, with its attendant gender, health, and age limitations, out of the picture."[39] The courage of the martyr is not a "courage" of codependency, but one that is grounded in love for

God, others, and oneself. This kind of courage is present in the person who faces a long terminal illness, as well as those who care for her. It is present in the person who endures the suffering brought on by a struggle with anxiety or depression. It is present in the person who faces a lifelong struggle with physical pain. It is present in nursing homes, hospital rooms, prisons, and hospice centers, and in the cardboard boxes that serve as shelter for the unhoused around the world. It is present in those who endure prejudice, oppression, and marginalization, and in those who struggle against these things in the name of justice and love.

Followers of the Way will be growing in courage, over time. But it won't be because they have technological advantages in warfare, greater physical strength, or a gun, or because they are self-sufficient protectors of themselves and those they love. Instead, they courageously carry a cross of self-denying love. They will be growing in courage because they have a deeper love for God, other human beings, and all of creation. As that self-denying and all-encompassing love of Christ grows in them, the courage that is dependent on such love will be able to grow as well. Love was at the center of Christ's life, making such courage possible. The same must be true of us, who seek to follow in his steps.

Love also undermines sin and the vices that produce it. For example, love is the spiritual antidote to sloth. We don't use this word much anymore. For years, I thought sloth (during those rare times that I actually thought about it) was just an older word for laziness. What first comes to your mind when you think of sloth? Binge-watching some series on Netflix or Hulu? That person at work who does all they can to avoid, you know, actually working? Or maybe the three-toed sloth, the slowest-moving mammal on the planet? Sloth can be manifested in laziness, but in the Christian tradition it is much more than that. In fact, we can exhibit the vice of sloth even if we are very busy and productive. How can that be? Sloth is best defined as resistance to the transformative demands of love.[40] Sloth is an indifference to the needs of others, our obligations to them, and how meeting these obligations requires us to change. This resistance to love's demands can show up as a kind of laziness. So binge-watching a show on your favorite streaming service can be an instance of sloth, if you do that instead of doing something for a friend or loved one that needs to be done.

Sloth can also manifest itself as a restless busyness. The workaholic who avoids the demands of love at work, at home, or with friends is actually being slothful. The person who scrolls through social media for hours fits here as well. They are doing something, but it's a pretty safe bet that it has little to do with the demands of love. Like many of us, I would guess, I can be slothful in both ways. There are times when I choose to do little or nothing when I have important responsibilities to fulfill. There are times when I definitely engage in a restless busyness, as a manifestation of anxiety and avoiding the demands of love, rather than trying to serve God and others.

Before we look at how love counteracts sloth, a couple of clarifications are needed. First, human beings need to rest. Rest is not slothful or lazy, if that is what we need.

And my guess is that most of us need more rest, or what used to be called leisure. We need time that is set aside for rest, recreation, and renewal in our relationships with God and others. And there isn't necessarily anything wrong with the occasional binge-watching of a show we like, within reason. Second, working hard doesn't entail that you are being slothful, exhibiting a restless busyness. Just like rest, hard work is good. But our motives matter. If we are allowing our work to keep us from what God might want to do in and through us, from loving him and others, then it is a barrier to spiritual growth, moral development, and contribution to the common good.

How do we know if sloth is a problem? Some of its symptoms include escapism, restlessness, and self-indulgence. So, do we run to TV shows, movies, social media, books, food, alcohol, or something else to escape our responsibilities in life? If so, then there's a good chance that sloth is at work (so to speak). We can use these things as ways to escape our responsibilities, to indulge our selfish desires, to avoid or resist the demands of love. We can even avoid the demands of love with religious activity. Think of the strained marriage where one or both spouses spend increasing amounts of time serving at church, rather than working at repairing and renewing their relationship.

Let's say we have identified that sloth is at least somewhat of a problem. What can we do about it? This is where love comes in.

First and foremost, we must open our hearts and minds to the love of God and seek to be intentional about responding to his transforming love. This includes his call to love others with the same self-giving love he shows to us. But we must regularly remind ourselves that we are loved by God just as we are. Anne Lamott is right when she tells us that "the secret is that God loves us exactly the way we are and that he loves us too much to let us stay like this,"[41] but it seems that this secret is difficult to accept. Some of us have a hard time really believing that God loves us right now, just as we are, and could not possibly love us more. This is the camp I'm in. For others, it is hard to believe that we can really change, that God can do something so that we don't stay like this. But wherever we are, we have to enter into the truth that God loves us and let it wash over and through us. The more we are permeated by the reality of God's love, the more we'll be able to submit to its transformative demands and push back against the power of sloth in our lives.

One way we can intentionally do this is by seeking to persevere in love in the daily opportunities we have to die to our selfishness, in the little details of life. In our relationships, it is often the small but meaningful choices that can make all the difference, and not only in the relationship but also in our character. Our love for a spouse or a good friend and our love for God "must be lived out over and over, day after day."[42] When we resist small acts of service, or kindness, or encouragement, we resist love. When we are alert to the small opportunities God brings our way, we can exemplify and grow in the virtue of love.

Another way to push back in love against sloth is to stay where we are. This might mean staying in a physical place, a place of one's calling and vocation, or both. For a few years after moving to Kentucky, we wanted to get out. It was culture shock, moving from southern California, to Boulder, Colorado, and then to a small town in central Kentucky. Half the time we couldn't understand what people were saying. It took a while to form new friendships in a place where people and their families had lived for generations. But we stayed, first by necessity and then by choice. Now we are very glad that we did. As human beings we sometimes want to flee our responsibilities, our relationships, our jobs, or our churches. But it is better to stay. Leaving can look better or easier, but it often isn't.

Live locally. God put me where I am; he put you where you are. Our primary responsibilities are to the people in our home, our church, and our community. Technology enables us to reach beyond those borders in our service, giving, and interactions. But I'm convinced that many of us focus too much on the world out there, rather than the world where we are. God may call you to another part of the city where you live, or to another part of our planet. Either way, that physical place is where your primary responsibilities lie. If I tweet eloquently about the gospel, social justice, apologetics, or politics but have not love for my family, friends, fellow believers, neighbors, and others in my community, I'm just a noisy gong and clanging cymbal.

Stay committed to your town, to your church, to those you love. There are exceptions, of course. We must be wise and flee when there is unchecked spiritual abuse in a church. Any kind of abuse in marriage or friendship— or in any relationship, for that matter—is unacceptable.

God can certainly call us to a new church, town, country, or vocation. But in other scenarios, we can defeat sloth and grow in love by simply choosing to stay.

Given the ways that love nourishes, fosters, and strengthens many virtues and how it undermines the vice of sloth, growth in love tends to foster growth in our overall character. Love fosters a wider and deeper growth in Christ. It is the roof that covers and protects a growing and healthy character, occurring within a growing and healthy relationship with Christ and his church.

## Conclusion

One of the most beautiful and striking pictures of the Way of humility and love in the Bible is found in the parable of the prodigal son (Luke 15:11–32). It's worth taking the time to read it in full:

> Then Jesus said, "There was a man who had two sons. The younger of them said to his father, 'Father, give me the share of the property that will belong to me.' So he divided his property between them. A few days later the younger son gathered all he had and traveled to a distant country, and there he squandered his property in dissolute living. When he had spent everything, a severe famine took place throughout the country, and he began to be in need. So he went and hired himself out to one of the citizens of that country, who sent him to his fields to feed the pigs. He would gladly have filled himself with the pods that the pigs were eating; and no one gave him anything.

But when he came to himself he said, 'How many of my father's hired hands have bread enough and to spare, but here I am dying of hunger! I will get up and go to my father, and I will say to him, "Father, I have sinned against heaven and before you; I am no longer worthy to be called your son; treat me like one of your hired hands."' So he set off and went to his father. But while he was still far off, his father saw him and was filled with compassion; he ran and put his arms around him and kissed him. Then the son said to him, 'Father, I have sinned against heaven and before you; I am no longer worthy to be called your son.' But the father said to his slaves, 'Quickly, bring out a robe—the best one—and put it on him; put a ring on his finger and sandals on his feet. And get the fatted calf and kill it, and let us eat and celebrate; for this son of mine was dead and is alive again; he was lost and is found!' And they began to celebrate.

"Now his elder son was in the field; and when he came and approached the house, he heard music and dancing. He called one of the slaves and asked what was going on. He replied, 'Your brother has come, and your father has killed the fatted calf, because he has got him back safe and sound.' Then he became angry and refused to go in. His father came out and began to plead with him. But he answered his father, 'Listen! For all these years I have been working like a slave for you, and I have never disobeyed your command; yet you have never given me even a young goat so that I might celebrate with my friends. But when this son of yours came back, who has devoured your property with prostitutes, you killed the fatted calf for him!' Then the father said to him, 'Son, you are always with me, and all that is mine is yours. But we had to celebrate and rejoice, because this brother of yours was dead and has come to life; he was lost and has been found.'"

For years I thought the focus of the parable was (1) the repentance of the prodigal son, who showed humility by returning home after insulting his family and squandering his inheritance; and (2) the pride of the other son who stayed and fulfilled his family responsibilities. Perhaps this had to do with self-centeredness and individualism that was lurking beneath the surface in how I read and understood the Bible. I often approached it as if it was about me, when it is actually about God and his kingdom. I have a role to play in that, as we all do; but as is often said, God is the main character in the narrative of the Bible. Not you. Not me. God.

Yet there is much for us to learn from these two characters in the parable. Time spent meditating and thinking about them—their hearts, their deeds, and the relevance of this for our own lives—is time well spent. The prodigal son exemplifies humility. In his poverty and need, he realizes the father he left can help him, so he returns home. His older brother exemplifies pride. He resents not getting what he feels he deserves. He resents the grace his brother is given. There is much to learn here. But I've benefitted from others who have shown that the primary lesson of the parable has more to do with what it says about the father.

In his book *The Return of the Prodigal Son*, Henri Nouwen shares the fruit of his extended meditations on the parable and on Rembrandt's painting from which the book's title is taken. The parable and the painting reveal to Nouwen a God of compassion and love. But there is another aspect of God's heart, one that is discussed here and there by Nouwen without being named. Nouwen talks about God being a father who runs out to meet his children, who "leaves the house, ignoring his dignity by running toward them."[43] The father of the prodigal is humble. He sets honor, dignity, and propriety aside and in humility runs to embrace his lost son in love. The humility of the son comes from desperation. The humility of the father is born out of love. Both kinds of humility are good, but the latter is better. The humility of the father is the humility of God. God, like the father in the parable, is concerned for his children, not himself; "he wants to give himself to them completely . . . to pour out all of himself . . . from a heart that does not demand anything for itself, a heart that is completely empty of self-seeking."[44] God's humility can be our humility, too. God's heart is a humble heart. Ours can be, too. We can give to others the humility and love that God gives to us. We can become people of the Way.

But to become people of the Way is not easy. The Way is not a path of triumphalism or worldly power and prestige. Instead, it is a downward path, as Marlena Graves makes clear: "There's always surrender to humiliation and crucifixion, an emptying, before the glory. There's no way around it. For my own part, I wish there were. Emptiness comes before fullness. We have to empty ourselves of anything that crowds out the life or grace of God in our lives. When we cooperate with the Spirit in this way, we become receptacles of grace. Like Jesus' mother Mary, we become God-bearers, pregnant with the divine. We are rich toward God and others. Filled full."[45]

I'm with Marlena Graves, as I suspect many of us are. Why can't we just have fullness in Christ immediately? Why do we have to become poor before we can become rich toward God and others? These questions raise other questions. The answers can be complex. As we ask questions and seek the answers, we must remember that our purpose is to become the kind of people who, by God's grace, become full in Christ and rich toward God and others. We can't skip over the emptying on our way to such glory.

Once we accept this reality, the next question is clear. How do we do this? How do we surrender? How do we become receptacles of grace? How, specifically, can we be intentional about our growth in humility and love as followers of the Way? These are the questions we'll explore next as we seek to become people of the Way.

four

# Practices of the Way

I t is not enough merely to *understand* humility and love. For those who want to grow in Christian virtue, in authentic Christlikeness, we must make actual progress in *being* more humble and loving. While this is a work of grace and of the Spirit of God, we have an important role to play. One way to intentionally cultivate these virtues is through practicing the classical spiritual disciplines of the Christian faith. In his day, Dietrich Bonhoeffer observed that "very widespread among Protestants is an inability even to understand the significance of disciplined practices, such as spiritual exercises, asceticism, meditation, and contemplation."[1] In my experience, this is still a problem not only for Protestants but for the church more generally, though there is a growing movement committed to these practices. Study, spiritual reading, prayer, fasting, silence, solitude, meditation, service, community, lament, and other spiritual disciplines are ways we can express humility and love as well as practices that can help us become more humble and loving.

These disciplines are important for followers of the Way. They are a means of God's transformative grace in our lives. When we are committed to practicing even a few of these, we open ourselves up to the work of the Holy Spirit in a variety of ways. Our union with God can be deepened. They can also help us to actually put into practice the words of Jesus. There are many excellent classic and contemporary writings on the disciplines that can be of use to us on this part of our journey along the Way.[2]

In many ways, this kind of spiritual growth is like growth as an athlete.[3] Imagine some young teenagers who want to be good at baseball. What do they do? When they play a baseball game, they imitate their favorite player. In my youth, we would imitate our favorite members of the Kansas City Royals: the hitting of George Brett, the base-stealing of Willie Wilson, or the fielding of Frank White. Our aspiring baseball stars might wear the same shoes as their baseball idol, buy the same glove, or hold their bat like him. But if all they do is try to be like him during a game, they'll never succeed. Elite athletes are able to perform at the level they do because they've practiced for hours upon hours, preparing their minds and bodies to do so, and organized much of their lives around their athletic goals. Daily habits practiced over years make the difference on game day, habits related not only to practicing the sport but also to diet, exercise, recovery, and sleep. Dallas Willard points out that this is a fundamental truth not only for athletes but also for musicians, surgeons, and teachers; it is actually a general principle that covers all of human life. In the heat of the moment, we have a much better chance of doing what we must if we have prepared for that moment by how we've lived each day. Applying this principle to the Christian life, Willard says, "Our mistake is to think that following Jesus consists in loving our enemies, going the 'second mile,' turning the other cheek, suffering patiently and hopefully—while living the rest of our lives just as everyone around us does. This is like the aspiring young baseball players mentioned earlier. It's a strategy bound to fail. . . . In truth *it is not the way of Christ* anymore than striving to act in a certain manner in the heat of a game is the way of the champion athlete."[4]

We must engage in a life where habitual practice of those spiritual disciplines that help us grow is the norm. When we do, we'll be ready when we are called upon to love an enemy, turn the other cheek, or endure suffering. We'll be ready to act in humble and loving ways because we'll actually be humble and loving.

For most of the disciplines discussed in this chapter, I'll make use of several key insights from Dietrich Bonhoeffer's book *Life Together*.[5] There are so many followers of the Way, past and present, who can help us with this aspect of the Christian life. My primary reason for selecting Bonhoeffer is that he offers us a much-needed perspective on spiritual disciplines *grounded in Christian community*. Bonhoeffer's thoughts will help us understand the centrality of several spiritual practices for growth in humility and love. And hopefully this discussion will move you to read Bonhoeffer's book for yourself!

In what follows, we'll take what we've learned about humility and love and explore some intensely practical advice on how to cultivate these virtues, how to participate more fully in the divine nature (2 Pet. 1:4), how to experience union with the Trinity, and how to practice unity in the body of Christ. We'll look at some of the classic spiritual disciplines, as well as a few others that aren't as widely discussed but are potentially very fruitful. We will do so with a special focus on how these disciplines relate to growth in humility and love. That is not all that they are good for, but they are most certainly good for that. Let's explore how.

## Community

Several years ago, we were part of a small local church with two lay leaders who had very different political perspectives. One was a conservative Republican. The other ran several campaigns for Democratic candidates. They not only got along; they were friends. Imagine that! This is the kind of community that humility and love can create in a church. Relationships within the church are one of the primary ways these virtues can be cultivated and exemplified. Our local church is for our character what a gym is for the body. The gym helps develop stronger muscles and better fitness; the church helps us develop the strength and fitness of character that are needed for followers of the Way. But too often we see pride, selfishness, callousness, and even hatred in the church. Politics, personalities, and trivialities can bring out the worst in us. Sadly, grievous sins like prejudice and physical, emotional, spiritual, and sexual abuse, including at times the protection of abusers and vilifying of the survivors of such abuse, are perpetrated in our midst. But at its best a church that is a truly Christian community can be a place of faith, hope, love, humility, compassion, and patience and a force for justice. It can be a place where all kinds of needs are met. It can be a place where people are known, a place where they love and are loved.

My wife and I are part of a new church plant. One of the first things our community did was read through and discuss portions of Bonhoeffer's *Life Together*. As I write this, our church has been meeting for public worship for about a year. Seeing some of what Bonhoeffer writes about life together as a community of Christians playing out in our church is one of the most meaningful things I've been a part of in the thirty-five years that I've been a follower of Jesus.

Bonhoeffer makes an observation that cuts to the quick of how a significant portion of the church in America approaches community, and also helps explain why it is perhaps rare. He writes, "Those who love their dream of a Christian community more than the Christian community itself become destroyers of that Christian community even though their personal intentions may be ever so honest, earnest, and sacrificial."[6] For all our talk of community, of "doing life together," as innumerable churches and ministries express, I fear that for myself and for many the dream of some ideal Christian community is undermining the actual formation of deep community in our churches. We have an ideal, which in and of itself is a good thing. We should strive for it in our life together. But Bonhoeffer is right: the ideal can also be harmful. If we relate to our community on the basis of what we demand from it, rather than as those who gratefully receive from it, we can harm it. This is so easy to do. The individualism of American society, coupled with the isolation brought on by the pandemic, has perhaps made many feel their need for community more deeply than before. But rather than coming from a place of demand, we should come from a place of gratitude. We need to turn outward, rather than inward, for "the Christian community has not been given to us by God for us to be continually taking its temperature."[7] This doesn't mean we should ignore or tolerate abuse, make excuses for those in positions of authority, or pretend things are better than they are. We can receive good things from our community with gratitude and hold it accountable with grace and truth, but we shouldn't approach it as consumers. There is so much more for us to give and receive in and through community. As a Christian, each one of us is to be "a physical sign of the gracious presence of the triune God."[8] As this becomes a greater reality in and through our Christian communities, and we become such signs not just to one another but also to the poor, the sick, the prisoner, the immigrant, the lonely, the oppressed, the marginalized, and everyone else, then we truly are bringing God's kingdom to bear in our world. We do this by loving others for who they are, not trying to control or coerce them into being who we think they should be. Bonhoeffer envisions a community of non-coercive love in which people are free to be Christ's, to be who they are in him.

It's important that Christians are a *physical* sign of God. This leads us to Bonhoeffer's vision of how the community spends its days. In short, the days are to be spent together. Literally. He tells us that the community should spend time worshiping together in the morning. This can include reading the Bible together, singing, and prayer. There are different forms of this for different communities. What matters is that it happens. When I first read this, I loved the idea, but it also seemed pretty unrealistic. Who has time for this?

This is one of the ways our church has applied Bonhoeffer's insights about community. As I mentioned in chapter 1, many of us live near each other in a particular part of our small city, within walking distance of several other members of our church. We don't do this daily as Bonhoeffer would prefer, but this summer we've been getting together in small groups once a week to read a psalm, discuss it, and pray together. It doesn't happen every week, but when it does I'm always grateful that I went. This is where being neighbors helps—the people in our group all live within a two- to three-minute walk of each other's houses. There is something about physical proximity that makes life together a more realistic goal. It actually happens in this and many other ways. This isn't the only form this practice can take, as Bonhoeffer points out. This kind of community will look different in Kansas City or Los Angeles compared to a small town in Kentucky. The important thing is to be intentional about finding a way to do something like this in our particular circumstances.

Physical proximity is helpful not only for participating in Christian community but also for opening it up to others who might want to join in. Living in the community you are trying to serve creates unique opportunities.

Our church is focused on the local university and on the downtown area, especially those suffering from poverty, lack of dignified work, and addiction. Small opportunities to do everyday small things for people in our town who need help more readily arise because we are physically present—opportunities to provide a listening ear, care for them in some small way, develop a friendship, or simply recognize their dignity as human beings. It isn't a one-way street, however. As a church, we are seeing that our pride, our façade of self-sufficiency, and our misguided beliefs about material poverty and wealth are all challenged as we enter into relationships with those who are materially poor. These relationships are good for all of us, wealthy, poor, and everything in between. They help all of us grow in humility and love.

Community is one of the primary ways humility and love can be cultivated and practiced. In many ways, these virtues are relational virtues. Think about when you share for the fourteenth time about your struggle with impatience, or when that person who rubs you the wrong way does that thing that really annoys you, or when you are that person with someone else. These are all prime opportunities to both show and develop humility and love. Both of these virtues are mentioned in Colossians 3:12–14, where Paul is urging the Colossian church to bear with each other, to grow in Christ *together*. If any church is going to be a community like this, one where there is forgiveness, patience, and unity, then humility and love must be present. A community will never outgrow the need for these virtues.

We should be intentional about growth in humility and love in community, in our church, because we cannot be followers of the Way on our own. Why? Katie Hays, pastor of Galileo Church in Fort Worth, Texas, gives a good answer. We "are not equipped to carry our half of a relationship with the Deity of the universe, or the Word-of-God-Enfleshed, all by our lonesome. God is *a lot*. God is too much for any one of us, which is why we need each other."[9] She is right. Alone we are too weak. When our faith falters, we need others to have faith for us. One way we stay connected to God is by our connection to our church, the body of Christ where we are. When we are struggling with our faith, with the trials of this life, this truth becomes more real. We see that we were never meant to try to make it through life in this fallen, broken, messed up, but still good and beautiful world alone with Jesus. We are image bearers of the Trinity. God is a fundamentally relational being, and we were made that way, too. Trying to go it alone cuts against the grain of our human nature, as God designed it. We cannot flourish alone. We need each other. We need to relate to each other in humility and love.

We can be intentional about growth in humility and love by asking God to give us an awareness of their importance in our church and in the work our church does in the community. We can ask God for the grace to show them to others (and ourselves) when it is really difficult to do so. And when we fall short, asking our brothers and sisters in Christ for forgiveness, when it is right to do so, will help us develop humility and love because the request for forgiveness is itself an act of humility and love.

## Scripture

As followers of Jesus, we "live entirely by the truth of God's Word in Jesus Christ" and thereby receive many spiritual benefits.[10] One mark of a spiritually healthy individual and a spiritually healthy community is that "the word of God is living and active" (Heb. 4:12) in that person and in that community. Bonhoeffer describes it well:

> When people are deeply affected by the Word, they tell it to other people. God has willed that we should seek and find God's living Word in the testimony of other Christians, in the mouths of human beings. Therefore, Christians need other Christians who speak God's Word to them. They need them again and again when they become uncertain and disheartened because, living by their own resources, they cannot help themselves without cheating themselves out of the truth. . . . The Christ in one's own heart is weaker than the Christ in the word of another Christian. The heart in one's heart is uncertain; the Word is sure.[11]

How can we become the kind of people who are "deeply affected by the Word"? How can we be influenced and changed by it? Certainly practices like reflective and prayerful reading by ourselves and with others are useful here, as are study, memorization, and meditation. All of these practices can have many positive effects, as we make space for the Word to be living and active in our lives, deepening our relationship with God in Christ.

It is important that we approach the Scriptures with an attitude of humility and love. Writing in the fifth century, theologian and monastic John Cassian explains it this way: "You must then, if you want to get at the true knowledge of the Scriptures, endeavour first to secure steadfast humility of heart, to carry you on by the perfection of love not to the knowledge which puffeth up, but to that which enlightens."[12] The importance of humility and love as we engage, interpret, and apply the words of the Bible is clear. It's a virtuous cycle. We come to the Bible with even a small bit of humility and love, and as we meet God there we understand him, including his humility and love, more deeply. By his grace, we're moved to be more like him, to be people of humility and love. As we do, we come to the Bible again with more humility and love, and the fruit is yet more humility and love. By his grace, the cycle repeats itself, and in the long run we become more Christlike.

I've found that memorizing Scripture can be helpful for growth in the virtues of humility and love. Memorization in general can be hard. This is humbling. It can also be an act of humility to memorize Scripture because we realize that we need to do this, that our flourishing is dependent on the truths revealed in God's word. There is a humility in recognizing that we are not self-sufficient, that our plans for growth will fall short unless they embody dependence on God. Memorizing Scripture is a way to cultivate and express this dependence. We need the renewal of heart and mind that memorizing Scripture can facilitate. In my own experience, having some passages committed to memory helps me to love God and others. In recent years, having the Lord's Prayer committed to memory has been important for my own life. Many times I just don't have the words to pray. I might be too tired, too discouraged, or simply at the end of my rope in the midst of some trial. In these moments, I use this prayer as a springboard for specific prayers. At other times, I just pray it word for word, as that is all I can do. When extemporaneous prayer is hard, and even when it isn't, we need the words of Scripture, memorized, to help us pray.

What about our need for other Christians to speak God's word to us? I'd like to begin with a confession. Or maybe it's a complaint. Actually, it's a bit of both. There is a part of me that resists what Bonhoeffer says here, given some of the experiences I've had over the years. A part of me doesn't want other Christians speaking God's word to me. But Bonhoeffer echoes the Bible here: "Let the word of Christ dwell in you richly; teach and admonish one another in all wisdom; and with gratitude in your hearts sing psalms, hymns, and spiritual songs to God" (Col. 3:16). So why do I resist this? Part of it is pride, perhaps a desire for independence as well. But my reticence also has to do with how some Christians go about speaking God's word to others. Too often we quote Scripture *at* each other. Too often we throw out a couple of proof texts that we think others need to hear and that we think should lead them to agree with our theological, ethical, or political position. I know I've been guilty of this over the years.

We need other Christians to speak God's word to us. This is unquestionably true. It can strengthen us, encourage us, and often give us the help we need. But we don't need them to do so, and we should not do so, in ways that are controlling or coercive. Bonhoeffer says that we must love others in a way that recognizes their freedom and rejects any attempt to control, coerce, or dominate.[13] Christ became human, lived, died, and rose again for people as they are. He offers them forgiveness as they are. He has prepared eternal life for them as they are. He won't leave us as we are, thankfully, but it isn't up to me to change someone else. Instead, I should respect the freedom others have in Christ, as people who belong to Christ. They don't belong to me. My job is not to make them into the person I think they should become, or that I think Christ wants them to become. Instead, I speak the word of Christ to them and relate to them through a spiritual form of love, a love that sees them from Jesus's perspective. This is one way in which he is the mediator between his followers. This kind of love rejects impersonal, crude, and coercive interference in the lives of our siblings in Christ. Love wants nothing to do with the pleasure of being pious. Instead, in humility and love, we share the word of God, but we also patiently let the other person sit with that word, even for a long time.

We try to fix each other with the word, as if just quoting the Bible at someone will make everything better. We give a small impromptu sermon and expect that to fix the problem. But that's not the way it works. Better to, as Bonhoeffer says, "speak to Christ about the other Christian more than to the other Christian about Christ."[14] I think one way to do this is to pray for others with the words of Scripture. This is another way to speak the word of Christ to our brothers and sisters. It is yet another way that Christ is a mediator between us and them. This requires faith in him, faith that he will act. It often requires waiting, which is an act of humility and a way to grow in it. Recognizing our limits as human beings and refusing to try to go beyond them can both express and strengthen humility in us. Praying Scripture for others is an act of love, as we pray for their good. Such prayer, then, helps us grow in these traits. It helps us grow in humility and love. It helps us grow as followers of the Way.

### Prayer

Many spiritual practices overlap. We've seen how practices related to both community and Scripture work in tandem. This is true of prayer as well. Bonhoeffer notes that "from ancient times in the church a special significance has been attached to the *praying of Psalms* together."[15] He goes on to offer some important advice for how to approach praying the Psalms in community. He interprets the Psalms as the prayers of Jesus. Jesus prays them, and he prays them through us as we pray the Psalms.

Yet particular psalms may not reflect our experience at a given moment. I may not be struggling with an enemy or the betrayal of a loved one, or God may seem clearly present to me and not hidden or silent. How, then, can I pray them authentically? I can do this when I realize that the prayers of the Psalms belong not just to me, but to the entire community, the entire body of Christ. Other members of the body are experiencing hostility from enemies, betrayal, and the hiddenness of God. I can pray the Psalms on their behalf, and they can do the same for me.

When we pray the Psalms, we enter into a school of prayer. Bonhoeffer explains how.[16]

First, we learn that prayer is to be done in Christ's name. This is not a phrase we tack on to the end of prayer, in some empty formulaic manner. Rather, it reminds us that our prayers are to be grounded in God's word, not our selfish desires. Humility and love are needed for this and will grow in us as we truly pray in Christ's name. We learn to put the interests of others before our own when our prayers for them and ourselves are grounded in the Word. We learn to place God and his kingdom before ourselves and our own little self-seeking monarchies. As we do this, we also grow in the virtue of love, of being disposed to work for the good of others, not only in prayer but also in our other deeds.

Second, in this school of prayer we learn what we ought to pray. This can be difficult, as the experience of the psalmist does not always map onto our own. We may struggle to pray along with the psalmist as he proclaims his innocence and righteousness before God. We know we are neither innocent nor righteous. Yet in Christ, and by Christ, we are. In Christ, and by Christ, we can pray along with the psalmist.

Bonhoeffer doesn't discuss this, but in recent years I've gone out of my comfort zone and followed the Psalms into prayers of lament. As someone who cares deeply about words, about thinking the right words, saying the right words, teaching the right words, and writing the right words, I usually tend to guard the words I employ in prayer. Rather than just honestly pouring out a complaint or lament to God, I'll censor myself, which amounts to denying reality as I experience it. Or I'll quickly follow a lament up by praying what I think I ought to pray, with the right words that I think God will approve of. But what if God just wants to hear what is actually going on in my soul, even if it's not what "should" be going on? What if his grace, mercy, and love can actually handle me as I am, rather than me as I think I ought to be? Lament is an act of humility. Truly honest prayer is, too. Admitting my weakness by expressing my actual feelings, my actual thoughts, and my actual desires, uncensored, to God is humbling. I want to be better than I am, but in humility I need to come to God as I am, a fallen, fallible, limited, and dependent human creature. Being more bluntly honest with God, removing my filter of propriety, still feels weird to me. I still experience guilt when I do this. But I'm working at it, persevering in it. The Psalms don't just show us how to do this; they show us that it's okay to do this. More than okay, they show us that it is something God wants. For this, we can be grateful.

Third, the Psalms teach us to pray together. When we pray, we join with the worldwide body of Christ, which is also at prayer. This enables us to go beyond our own concerns and pray more selflessly, again reflecting the expansive humility and love of Christ as we do so. In this way, we can see that Bonhoeffer is right to conclude that "the more deeply we grow into the Psalms and the more often we ourselves have prayed them, the more simple and rewarding will our praying become."[17] Simple prayer is good. Through it, we experience the reward of a deeper union with God, but also the reward of growth in humble love.

There are temptations here for followers of the Way. René Padilla urges those who are committed to working and praying for God's kingdom to come on earth to recognize that Christ's kingdom is here, but also hidden. The earth is cursed, yet good. So much good is possible, here and now. When we recognize this, it "enables us to pray for the coming of the Kingdom as people who are fully on earth, without trying to avoid the misery, the hunger and the death of this cursed earth, while simultaneously not expecting to build a utopia of God's Kingdom on Earth. . . . 'Thy Kingdom come' . . . is the prayer of those who, on this accursed earth, wait for God's authentic miracle—the miracle of the God who brings life out of death."[18] We realize in humility that we cannot change the world, or the world in us. But as we pray, work, and wait, in partnership with God, change, however slow, sometimes comes. God can bring life out of death in the world, and he can do the same in us. Praying the Psalms can be helpful here, too. Often the psalmist cries out to God but then reminds himself in prayer of God's goodness, faithfulness, and love. Misery doesn't have the last word; mercy does. The Fall doesn't have the last word; the faithfulness of God does. The wait may be long, usually longer than we want, but we wait in hope. This hopeful waiting is also an act of humility and love; it is yet another way to grow in these virtues.

If our prayers are not reflecting humility and love, if they are not helping us become people of humility and love, then we might ask God and a few people we trust why this is. Some sort of change may be needed. God will be faithful to change us through the Holy Spirit and others in our Christian community. It won't be an easy question to ask, and the answers might be hard to hear, but a deeper union with God and a character more reflective of Jesus are worth it.

## Solitude

In his reflections on solitude, Bonhoeffer makes two important points: "Whoever cannot be alone should beware of community. Whoever cannot stand being in community should beware of being alone."[19]

If we cannot bear to be alone, if our experiences in solitude are uncomfortable or even painful, it is tempting to seek an escape through community. But the testimony of those who have persevered in solitude reveals that it is worth the struggle. Solitude can be a place of healing, a place of transformation, a place of deeper connection to God. Bonhoeffer goes on to say that for a person who can't bear being alone, fleeing solitude and seeking community will actually bring harm to them and that community. Bonhoeffer's warning here is apt for those who tend to avoid what is going on inside of them, the hard stuff that can more easily bubble to the surface in times of solitude. If we refuse to deal with it, if we refuse to allow God to work on it in our time alone with him, then we may block the transformation God wants for us. And then we bring that hard stuff into the community and do it harm, often through an unhealthy set of expectations or demands that the community wasn't built to meet. For Bonhoeffer, part of the Christian life is done alone. I must choose to take up my cross, I must go through struggles, I must pray alone. I cannot avoid myself. If I try to do so I will harm myself and my community.

But if we enter into and remain in solitude, it can help us grow in humility and love, which is healing to us. It is humbling to become aware of what is going on beneath the surface. This is an awareness that solitude can produce. It is humbling to see the ways that we are broken, or sinful, or falling short in our key commitments to ourselves, others, and God. It is humbling to see the depths of our anger, or fear, or anxiety. But if we allow God's love to shatter our pride, we can be transformed as we humbly receive the good God has for us. It is only by allowing this awareness to surface that we can more fully experience the richness of God's grace, which itself deepens our experience of God's humility and love. Solitude opens us up to these sorts of experiences. And when we have such experiences, one result is that we are encouraged to grow in humility as well as love for God, others, and ourselves. In these ways solitude is good for us. When we bring this into our relationships with others, it is also good for the community.

If we cannot bear being in community, if our experiences there are uncomfortable, discouraging, or even painful, it is tempting to seek an escape through being alone. But this is a mistake because we are called into a community of faith. I carry my cross, I struggle, I pray, but I do this with others in my community. For Bonhoeffer, if I neglect the community of faith I neglect Christ.

If I do this, solitude becomes harmful to me, because I'm putting distance between myself and Christ rather than engaging him in it.

We've already discussed community and how it fosters growth in humility and love. Let's turn to specific practices of solitude and consider how they can foster such growth. Before we do, it is important to note that Bonhoeffer believes that "the mark of solitude is silence."[20] I think he is right. Solitude and silence don't have to go together, but they are a natural pair of practices to try in tandem.

When I first tried to implement solitude and silence into my days, one thing that was helpful was to set a timer for ten to thirty minutes and just do nothing, alone in a quiet room. No agenda and no expectations (which can be hard, because we want to *experience* God). The simple act of being alone, away from people, screens, noise, demands, and other responsibilities, really is life-giving.

More recently, I've been using an app called "Centering Prayer," which walks you through some guided time in solitude with God. You select a word that expresses your intention for your time alone with God and use it to focus and refocus yourself. In recent months I've focused on "faith" pretty consistently, as life seems to be testing and trying my faith a lot these days. I especially appreciate the quote from Thomas Keating that pops up after the time of solitude: we should "persevere in contemplative practice without worrying about where we are on the journey."[21] If we just surrender to God, reject the temptation to compare ourselves with others, and trust that the fruit of our time alone may be hidden from us, as Keating advises, then we are free to just be. We are free to trust God where we are and where he is taking us. Bonhoeffer concurs, advising that the silence of Christians "will be richly rewarded if they do not set any conditions on how they expect this encounter to take place or what they hope to get from it, but simply accept it as it comes."[22]

This is hard for me. I want results; I want to have these deep and rich experiences of God. But I'm learning to put the evaluations and demands aside and to simply be with God. These small acts of faithfulness matter. Whether or not I have some incredible, life-altering, deep experience of God, I'm learning that I may be experiencing more change, and more of God, than I realize. It may be in small doses, but over time I believe that my relationship with God and others is growing deeper. I hope so. I think so.

While solitude can help us grow in self-knowledge, another way to practice it has more to do with our knowledge and experience of God. As Dallas Willard describes it, in our time alone with God "it is possible to have silence, to be still, and to *know* that Jehovah is indeed God (Ps. 46:10), to set the Lord before our minds with sufficient intensity and duration that we stay centered on him—our hearts fixed, established in trust (Ps. 112:7–8)—even when back in the office, shop, or home."[23] This practice of solitude can help us grow in humility, as God becomes our central focus rather than ourselves and our desires. To focus our attention, our very selves, on God is an act of humility and strengthens this virtue in us. When we enter into times of solitude and silence as times to intentionally set God before our minds, it trains us in the other-centered aspect of humility because we are thinking about God rather than ourselves. We can take that focus into the substance of everyday life and relate to others in humility, too. This is a fruit of focusing on God in solitude.

What about the silence we offer and experience in solitude? How can that help us grow in humility?[24] One form of silence is withdrawal from the noise of the world, the screens, the people, the near-constant din of distraction. Another kind of silence is that of simply not speaking, which we can take with us out of our time of solitude into our daily lives as appropriate. The point is not that we entirely refrain from speaking at all, though there may be times for this. Rather, it is that we engage in a particular kind of silence, namely, we forgo the practice of trying to gain the approval of others with our words.[25] This is a way to cultivate humility, as we become less dependent on the approval or praise of others. Approval and praise are good things, of course, but if we need them too much we are allowing others to dictate our value to us. This form of silence is also a way to cultivate love. When I talk less and listen more, I communicate to others that I value them; I care about them and what they think. I love by listening, and I listen in love.

## Service

Bonhoeffer contends that God's mercy is the foundation of the spiritual discipline of service.[26] He believes that our experience of mercy creates in us a desire to serve. At the outset, then, humility comes into play. To receive mercy we must be humble; we must admit that we are in need of mercy. In order to learn to serve, Bonhoeffer says that we must learn to think little of ourselves. And as we serve, we should put the will of our neighbor above our own will. We also value their honor more than our own. All of this requires and manifests humility. To follow Christ in service, we must also do so in love. Humility and love are present in service to the community and are formed in members of that community through service. Bonhoeffer describes several forms of service that we owe to each other.

The first service we owe to others (including God) in our community is *listening to them*. We experience God's love and learn to love God by listening to his word. We learn to love other people by listening to their words. But all too often we prefer talking to listening. We would rather tell people what we think, what we feel, what they should think, and what they should feel, rather than offering them the simple service of a listening ear. This is lethal to the spiritual life, according to Bonhoeffer. When followers of Jesus are unable to listen to one another, we soon lose our ability to listen to God. We then incessantly talk to God but do not give him the time and space to speak to us, so that "in the end there is nothing left but empty spiritual chatter and clerical condescension which chokes on pious words."[27] Often, when we do listen to others, it is "with half an ear that presumes already to know what the other person has to say."[28] This counterfeit listening reveals our impatience and self-centeredness. It short-circuits the formation of a community of humble love. We can do better, of course, in forming and strengthening such a community. One significant step in this direction is to simply learn to listen to God and others, attentively, patiently, humbly, and lovingly.

The second service we owe to others in our community is *active helpfulness*. Here Bonhoeffer has in mind the little acts of service in a community where life together is truly valued. Whether it is giving someone a ride to an appointment, making a meal for a family, helping someone do their taxes, or the myriad little acts of service that meet the needs of others, all of it matters. Bonhoeffer connects this kind of service to both humility and love. Being ready to alter our plans, set aside our "important" tasks or projects, including our "religious" or "spiritual" ones, in order to serve others in such ways is "part of the school of humility."[29] Pride tells us that we have too much that is important to do, that can't be set aside for meeting the needs of someone else. Humility leads us to set these things aside and serve others. These little everyday acts of service are also important because they are, at bottom, acts of love. We don't want to be like the priest or Levite who passed by the wounded man on the side of the road. Followers of the Way will be like the good Samaritan, moved with compassion to show mercy as we help those in need (Luke 10:25–37).

Finally, there is the service of *bearing with others*. We fulfill the law of Christ by bearing each other's burdens (Gal. 6:2). Other people are a burden to followers of Jesus that we willingly, humbly, and lovingly bear. They are a burden in the sense that we endure and suffer with them. Interestingly, Bonhoeffer points to the freedom of others as a burden we must bear. Rather than coercively trying to make people into our image, we are to give others the freedom to become who they are, for God to create his image in them as he sees fit. We might begin by simply "tolerating the reality of the other's creation by God," but we must move beyond mere toleration to affirming this fact, even "breaking through to delight in it."[30] This is no easy task. Others irritate us, see things differently than us, and misuse their freedom in various sinful ways. Bearing with them requires patience when irritated, forgiveness when wronged, a humility that rejects judgment, and a love that covers a multitude of sins. We need others to be patient, forgiving, humble, and loving with us. They need the same from us. As we serve one another in these ways, we serve the community, and it becomes the kind of place that is characterized by love and humility. It becomes the kind of place that shows others the Way. More than that, it invites them more fully and deeply into that Way.

### Just Peacemaking

Peacemaking and justice are deeply interconnected. Any peace worth having must be a just peace. There are many different aspects of just peacemaking. There are better and worse ways to pursue peace. Followers of the Way pursue nonviolent solutions to our conflicts, whether political or personal. Martin Luther King explains it this way: "Nonviolence is the answer to the crucial political and moral question of our time—the need for man to overcome oppression and violence without resorting to violence and oppression . . . man must evolve for all human conflict a method which rejects revenge, aggression, and retaliation. The foundation of such a method is love."[31]

Pacifists like Martin Luther King argue that violence is the way of the world, not the way of Christ and his kingdom. They make use of the many biblical texts that support this view (Matt. 5:38–39, 43–45; Rom. 12:18–21; 2 Cor. 10:3–4; 1 Pet. 2:21–23; among many others). They believe that in following the Prince of Peace a commitment to peace is nonnegotiable.

Followers of the Way are to be peacemakers; they work for peace. Like Martin Luther King, they see that peacemaking can happen only if love is at the foundation of who they are and what they do. They pursue peace, even at great costs to themselves. They realize that their commitment to peace may cost them a lot, even their very lives. They practice peace and reject the quick turn to violence, a path that so many follow. Jesus blesses the peacemakers in the Sermon on the Mount (Matt. 5:9). He commands us to love our enemies there, too (Matt. 5:44). Peace is a fruit of the Spirit (Gal. 5:22–23). And Romans 12:18 sets a high standard: "If it is possible, so far as it depends on you, live peaceably with all." Peacemakers take these Scripture passages, and many others like them, with utmost seriousness and are committed to living out these values in their daily lives.

Any peace worth having must be a just peace. There are many different aspects of just peacemaking. Racial realities in America right now cry out for justice and peace. In a discussion of the pursuit of racial justice, Malcolm Foley points out how the Scriptures teach us to approach these issues. He says we must engage in what he calls "active peacemaking."[32] To be an active peacemaker, we must not make the mistake of thinking that being color-blind will get us where we need to be, where we ought to be. For there to be deep harmony and true racial justice, those who are non-Black must *see* our Black brothers and sisters; we must see that they are forced to navigate the world differently if they want to survive. As Foley puts it, "If you are blind to my Blackness, you are blind to me."

But we must not be blind to anyone. If we are blind to someone, then we cannot love them. And love them we must:

> Love of neighbor begins with the recognition of the worth of our neighbor as well as a recognition of their struggles. In order to do that, however, my white brothers and sisters must recognize that the Black experience of the US is markedly different from their own. My white brothers and sisters must recognize that, as Dr. King said, "for the good of America, it is necessary to refute the idea that the dominant ideology in our country even today is freedom and equality while racism is just an occasional departure from the norm on the part of a few bigoted extremists." Racism is unfortunately not a localized malady; it is a systemic one, spreading through the bloodstream in a way that is not easily excised. But it is nonwhite communities that see and feel it most deeply.[33]

The problem is that our racialized society, with its embedded white supremacy, not only wrongly encourages us to be colorblind; it encourages us to be blind to the suffering and injustices that Black people and other people of color endure. It is difficult to excise it from our national bloodstream. The ideal of colorblindness exacerbates this. There are other ways we can, willfully or not, be blind to the suffering and struggles of our neighbors, ways that keep us from loving as we should. The demonization of critical race theory, and the strange hyperfocus that many have given to it, is one example of this. I think Christians are better off looking at the societal realities that gave birth to critical race theory and, decades later, Black Lives Matter, rather than hyperfocusing our critical gaze on this theory and this movement. No theory or movement is above criticism, of course, but when that becomes the primary or even sole focus, rather than the persisting injustices, something is wrong. We must try to see it. This requires humility. We must show it.

But it is not enough just to see injustice, or just to see our brothers, sisters, and neighbors and their suffering. We must do something about it. And what we must do, as Foley points out, is love. Cornel West puts it beautifully when he says that "justice is what love looks like in public." Love, including how it is manifested in just peacemaking, is how the world will know we are followers of the Way ( John 13:34–35). It is also how we will achieve both genuine unity in the body of Christ (Gal. 3:26–29) and a more righteous world where justice rolls down like water (Amos 5:24).

## Learning from the Marginalized

In the early months of the Covid-19 pandemic, I participated in a webinar on the ethics and theology of gun violence in the context of the pandemic.[34] During this panel, I expressed my hope that the rest of the church in America would take the opportunity to learn from the Black church, which for generations has exemplified so well how to hold fast to Christ and one another in the midst of suffering. The Black church is used to an experience of the faith where the Psalms matter in a deep way, resonating deeply with their experience of life and God, as it has cried out for justice and against oppression for hundreds of years. The suffering caused by slavery, Jim Crow, and the continued existence of both systemic and personal racism is obviously monumentally worse than the suffering caused by the pandemic. Yet it would have been so good to see more of the American church bear up under the suffering caused by the pandemic, suffering that was beyond our control, by holding fast to Christ and one another and loving our neighbor. Many chose just such a path. Sadly, many others chose a different path. Instead of learning how to suffer and care for others, some chose to resist wearing masks. Many embraced bizarre conspiracy theories about vaccines, the virus, and how to treat it. They chose to hold fast to their purported rights rather than focusing on their actual responsibilities to care for others. As a result, more people have died than would have otherwise been the case. But we don't need to depend on a pandemic to learn from the Black church. We can be intentional and start doing so now.

I'm speaking here to those of us who are given privilege in our society—of race, of power, of wealth, of comfort, of affirmation—though all Christians in all communities can apply what follows to their particular context.

In his book *The Color of Compromise*, Jemar Tisby offers several practical ways to deal with racial injustice in America.[35] One of his suggestions is that the rest of the American church should learn from the Black church. Tisby observes that Black theology has been devalued and is assumed to be heterodox or heretical in many white Christian spaces. My own experience bears this out. One of my graduate degrees is from a fairly conservative evangelical seminary. It was a philosophy degree, but we were also required to take a good deal of theology and biblical studies courses. I can't recall a course where we weren't allowed to explore or challenge any idea, but I also don't recall reading anything from the perspective of liberation theology (broadly conceived to include Black and feminist theology). We read about it, but we didn't actually read it. And that's a problem. What is seen as worthy of attention says a lot. In one of the systematic theology texts that we used, liberation theology was described as unorthodox. Such hasty generalizations should be avoided not only because they are false but also because they effectively discount important voices.

What should we do in such a situation? One place to start is to heed Tisby's advice: "the body of believers should commit themselves to valuing and learning from the distinct contributions that come from marginalized groups such as black people in America."[36] He then points out that by doing this, the rest of the church in

America could learn how to lament. Black Christians in America have suffered through the sustained evil of slavery and continue to suffer from the evils of injustice, bigotry, and marginalization. Tisby observes that the Black church has learned how to lament and how to turn sadness into strength. He goes on to say that the rest of the church could learn how to rejoice from the Black church. The vocal and exuberant joy of engaging in worship and experiencing God's goodness with one's whole self could revitalize and revive the rest of the church in beautiful ways. We need voices giving us interpretations and applications of the Bible that are grounded in the experiences of Black people in America.

Vincent Bacote, a theologian at Wheaton College, echoes Tisby's points about lament and emphasizes the cultivation of hope in the Black church that has occurred in the midst of great suffering and injustice.[37] The image of drawing from a deep well, where we can find the hard-won wisdom of the Black church, is a beautiful image to have in mind as one branches out and imbibes the wisdom of the Black church, as well as other marginalized groups in America. But there is something else for the rest of the church to learn from the Black church— the example it sets in discipleship. Bacote shares survey data that reveals some of the differences between how Black and white Christians approach discipleship. White Christians are more likely to see discipleship as the process of achieving spiritual goals, whereas Black Christians focus on character development in Christ. White Christians take an individualistic approach to spiritual growth, while Black Christians tend to see growth happening in the context of community. Black Christians are twice as likely as white Christians to currently be discipled by another follower of Christ. They are also more likely to be involved in discipling other Christians, to prefer group-based discipleship, and to see such groups as well as family members as very important to their spiritual growth. Black Christians are more likely to have a higher view of the truth of the Bible, more frequently study the Bible, and are nearly three times more likely to memorize Scripture than white Christians. They are also more likely to connect spiritual growth with social change.

In humility, the rest of the American church ought to be chastened by the faithfulness of the Black church and challenged to follow their example as they follow the example of Christ (1 Cor. 11:1). The rest of us ought to more faithfully follow the path they have set for the American church in loving God, our neighbors, and our enemies.

Seeking the wisdom of the marginalized is an act of humility, and it is an act of love. Taking the posture of a learner requires humility, as we admit our own lack of knowledge and our need for others to help us learn and grow. For those of us who are part of traditions that at best minimize and at worst vilify Black theology, we need to speak less and listen more. Yes, I see the irony present as I offer this advice in a book! But during the past few years I've been more intentional about listening and learning from different marginalized communities; these have been fruitful practices in my life. Such learning is also an act of love because in so doing we are recognizing the value of what the marginalized have to offer, giving them the respect they deserve. Simply listening to and learning from someone can be an act of love. As we cultivate humility and love in this practice of learning from the marginalized, I believe that new vistas of these virtues will open up, and we'll become more like the humble and loving Christ we seek to follow.

I'm at the beginning stages of this practice, but I will suggest a few books and authors that I think are good places to start, though they are not representative of all the marginalized communities in our nation and world. Tisby's *The Color of Compromise* as well as his more recent *How to Fight Racism*, Esau McCaulley's award-winning *Reading While Black: African American Biblical Interpretation as an Exercise in Hope*, and *Fortune* by Lisa Sharon Harper are all helpful for this practice of learning from the marginalized. Books from the past have much to teach us, too. *The Autobiography of Malcolm X*, Harriet Jacobs's *Incidents in the Life of a Slave Girl*, and various writings by Frederick Douglass and Martin Luther King Jr. will repay the time and effort spent reading them.

You will be challenged, you will learn, and you will grow if you open yourself up to understanding the experiences and ideas present in these (and many other) books in a spirit of humility and love. Reading and heeding the voices of the marginalized is a neglected practice that can help all of us rediscover the Way, as it has been embodied for centuries among the marginalized and oppressed communities who have remained faithful in following Christ with humility and love.

## Rhetorical Nonviolence

Humility and love lead us to act in ways that put the interests of others ahead of our own. One reason to live in this sacrificial way is that it leads to greater unity with others.[38] Yet all too often in our conversations with others, humility and love are conspicuously absent. Rather than humble love of truth, hope for furthering the common good, and concern for unity, our speech is marked by the prideful goal of embarrassing our opponent while exalting ourselves and our viewpoints, with a "certainty" that is immune to counterevidence and incapable of simple charity. Ultimately, and unsurprisingly, this leads to deep divisions.

Polarization is a growing problem. It is present in our attitudes and in the sharpness of our disagreements.[39] The number of people with consistently conservative or liberal positions has doubled since 1994. Our feelings about and views of people on the other side of many issues have become increasingly negative. *They* must be immoral, irrational, or not really Christian. We can't or won't see that they might have some good reasons for what they believe, or that their disagreement with us does not make them an unfaithful Christian or a bad person.

We all have experiences with the problem of polarization. It is in our homes, at the holiday dinner table, at church, at work, and on social media. When anger gets added to the mix, the results are worse. We show disdain for others. We dehumanize them. For what? For having a different view than we do? For refusing to toe the party line at school, work, or church? Anyone who reflects upon the state of our civil discourse can easily see these problems. I have seen a seminary-educated professing Christian offer the following reply, on social media, to several plans and policies of "the left" (tearing down certain statues, moving the United States of America away from his preferred values, and renaming John Wayne Airport in southern California), with the following refrain: "GO TO HELL."

It is easy to think that "these are just words, they don't cause much harm," or "People need to be tougher," or "Mean tweets are no big deal," but in the Sermon on the Mount Jesus rejects such justifications. He refuses to minimize the harm that angry words do: "You have heard that it was said to those of ancient times, 'You shall not murder'; and 'whoever murders shall be liable to judgment.' But I say to you that if you are angry with a brother or sister, you will be liable to judgment; and if you insult a brother or sister, you will be liable to the council; and if you say, 'You fool,' you will be liable to the hell of fire" (Matt. 5:21–22). It is clear that vicious anger and words spoken in such a spirit to others are to be taken very seriously.

We all have witnessed, experienced, or engaged in discourse that is uncivil, insulting, or characterized by vicious anger. I have witnessed it, engaged in it, and been on the receiving end of it. People to the right of me politically have told me that I have imbibed "the liberal Kool Aid" because I take a moderate position on how we can reduce gun violence in the United States of America.[40] Others have questioned my commitment to Christ because my website does not have the word "Jesus" displayed prominently on its homepage. I have also experienced disdain from those to the left of me politically, who have told me it's good that I live in Kentucky since I have such backward views about God and politics. Honestly, this kind of thing used to bother me a lot, given my personality and emotional makeup. But over time I have learned to handle it better, minimizing the mental and emotional space I give such comments. To be sure, this kind of feedback should be expected, insofar as I sometimes write about controversial issues. But whether we are witnessing it, are on the receiving end of it, or are perpetrating it, such verbal behavior is out of bounds. As James 3:10 tells us, "From the same mouth come blessing and cursing. My brothers and sisters, this ought not to be so."

What if more of us who follow Christ set a different standard? What if we took the words of James to heart? What if we followed the example of Christ himself? "When they hurled their insults at him, he did not retaliate; when he suffered, he made no threats. Instead, he entrusted himself to him who judges justly" (1 Pet. 2:23 NIV). Why was he able to respond in this way? There are many reasons, but among them is the fact that humility and love were and are central virtues in the character of Christ. In humble love, he refused to respond to insults and suffering at the hands of others with insults or threats. Instead, humility and love led him, and ought to lead us, to adopt a practice of rhetorical nonviolence.

What is rhetorical nonviolence? Let's begin with a general definition of nonviolent action: "Nonviolence is not passive nonresistance; nor is coercion always violent. Nonlethal coercion (as in a boycott or peaceful march) that respects the integrity and personhood of the 'opponent' is not immoral or violent. By 'nonviolent action,' I mean an activist confrontation with evil that respects the personhood even of the 'enemy' and therefore seeks both to end the oppression and to reconcile the oppressor through nonviolent methods."[41] This is consistent with the words of Jesus when he instructs his followers, "Do not resist an evildoer" and turn the other cheek (Matt. 5:39). A close study of the Greek word translated as "resist" here reveals that Jesus is not prohibiting all forms of resistance. Rather, he is prohibiting violent resistance. This is because the term "means to resist violently, to revolt or rebel, to engage in armed insurrection."[42] Nonviolence is not passivity. It is a form of activism that rejects violence as a means to achieving its goal. I am not a pacifist, but I'm very close to being one. A defense of nonviolence as a Christian doctrine, as well as a defense of its effectiveness, is beyond the scope of this book, but there is much good evidence, past and present, for both its truth and its effectiveness.[43] Of course, nonviolent resistance is not always effective, but for followers of the Way faithfulness, not effectiveness, should be our key concern.

If we apply this to how we speak to one another, we can understand rhetorical nonviolence as verbal behavior that reflects, in both content and tone, a respect for

one's opponent as a person made in God's image, reject-
ing insult and vicious anger, with a goal of coming to
know and apply the truth in unity. Only through humility can we approach those we disagree with in a spirit of
openness and willingness to be corrected. In humility,
we put truth and the good of our dialogue partner at the
center, rather than ourselves, our reputations, and our
desire to win. We may, of course, be right, and we must
resist what we believe is false. We should not be passive.
We can be right, resist what is false, and fight for truth,
goodness, justice, and beauty as we engage in debate and
dialogue with others. But we can interact with others—
both fellow Christians and those who do not share our
faith—in ways that reflect humility and love, rather than
pride and vicious anger.

It is right to do this. It is also effective. The words of
Proverbs 15:1 are actually true: "A gentle answer turns
away wrath, but a harsh word stirs up anger" (NIV). In
the past several years, I have tried to adopt this approach
of rhetorical nonviolence. I have not done so perfectly,
but I have made progress. I have seen several benefits to
doing so. First, it is one way that I can express love for
God and others. My experiences in working at this have
made a difference, not just in the tone of my interactions
with others when we disagree, but also in the substance.
It is incredible to see how a humble and loving response
to someone else's adversarial tone, or even an angry or
insulting tone, can change the dynamics of a conversation. I have seen this for years in the classroom and in
in-person discussions, but it also works in social media
interactions. Instead of firing back, we can ask a question,

see if there is common ground, or simply ask someone why they believe what they do, in a genuinely curious way. Instead of being opponents or enemies, we try to become partners in the quest for truth. Rhetorical non-violence opens the door for better conversations, softens my opponent's heart as well as my own, and refocuses the conversation on the substance of our discussion. If we truly desire and seek after truth, then this approach can help us get there.

I am not advising that we always do this. Rhetorical nonviolence is not a principle or rule we must always follow. If we understand it as such, we ignore the need for resistance to oppression and injustice, which can and at times should include righteous anger. We risk accepting injustice when instead it should be denounced and defeated. There are times when hard truths must be communicated in hard ways. Those who are victims of injustice and oppression, and their allies, should not be silenced in the name of rhetorical nonviolence.

What I am suggesting is that rhetorical nonviolence can be helpful to many as a worthwhile spiritual practice that can reshape our hearts and our relationships with others. For too many of the privileged, there is too much anger, too much verbal vitriol, too much pride, and not enough humble love expressed in being quiet and genuinely listening to others. There is a time and place for arguments. There is a time and place for strong words denouncing evil, injustice, and oppression. We need wisdom and sensitivity to discern this, and to discern how to interact in humility and love, regardless of the circumstances, in the Way of Jesus.

## Conclusion

These practices of the Way can help us become the people we are meant to be, the people we long to be. That is important. But they are not merely about us. They will help us experience the abundant life Christ came to give us, but they do more than that. When we grow in humility and love, we become the kind of people who exemplify a way of life that will draw others in. When they see the glimmers of the humility and love of Christ in our lives, others will want to join us on the Way, making progress on their own journey into the heart and life of Christ, in humility and love.

five

# *Preparing the Way*

We are not merely followers of the Way. We should also be preparers of the way to the Way. To be a follower of the Way *is to be* a preparer of the way to the Way, whether we know it or not, and whether we accept it or not. Thankfully, we see followers of Christ with beautiful character who consistently love and serve both God and others. While the faith of others is not our sole responsibility, we can help prepare the way for them to join with us on the Way. Sadly, we also see Christians who act as barriers to faith. Sometimes, the same people do both. Sometimes you do both. So do I. But we can do better, as we become more faithful to Christ in humility and love.

Many point toward the hypocrisy of Christians as a reason why they reject the faith. Others have left the faith for this reason. If we want to be disappointed in Christians, looking for varying degrees and types of hypocrisy among those who profess faith in Christ, the search won't take long. I used to think that the mistake here was looking at Christians, rather than Christ. If people could just focus on him, on his love, mercy, grace, and utter lack of hypocrisy, they would find good reasons to follow him. I still think there is something to this. Christ is the focus of our faith, not humans who fail to live up to his call on our lives.

But recently I've come to see this differently. I now empathize more with those who reject Christ because of Christians, for several reasons. First, I've seen the impact of hypocrisy in the hearts and minds of people I love. Second, wise words from Dietrich Bonhoeffer about how Christians must work at preparing the way for others have helped change my perspective. And third, Romans 2 explicitly addresses this issue in ways that I've missed seeing until recently.

Let's start with Romans 2. If I see myself as "a guide to the blind, a light to those who are in darkness, a corrector of the foolish, a teacher of children" (vv. 19–20) and yet fail to live up to my own professed beliefs—doing what I condemn others for—then I dishonor God and his name is blasphemed *because of me*. Paul goes on to talk about true spirituality being a matter of the heart. It is certainly demonstrated in actions, but it starts in the heart, where the Spirit of God dwells. No one is perfect. We all fall short in many ways. But we can be imperfect without being hypocritical. We should strive to avoid the sin of hypocrisy for our sake and the sake of others. This is yet another reason to pursue the virtues of humility and love.

In his magisterial work *Ethics*, Bonhoeffer discusses how Christians can prepare the way for others to receive God's grace.[1] He refers to justification by grace and by faith as *ultimate*. This is how we enter the Way. In contrast to this, examples of the *penultimate* include *food* for the hungry, *shelter* for the unhoused, *justice* for those whose rights are denied, *community* for the lonely, *order* for the undisciplined, and *freedom* for the slave. For those Christians who think we are obligated merely to share the good news about the forgiveness of sins given in Christ but not to address social ills and injustices, Bonhoeffer offers an important challenge. He argues that when "a human life is deprived of the conditions that are part of being human, the justification of such a life by grace and faith is at least seriously hindered, if not made impossible."[2] Those who share the good news of grace and forgiveness through faith must do all they can to gain it a hearing; they must prepare a way for people to hear and understand the relevance of that news. Ultimately, God is the one who clears the path. God makes a way for humans to come to him in faith. Yet, as Bonhoeffer also points out, we can oppose God's work and hinder the human response to God by what we do or fail to do. As Christians, the power of God in Christ to draw people to himself "does not release us from preparing the way for the coming of grace, from doing away with whatever hinders and makes it more difficult. . . . We can make it hard for ourselves and others to come to faith. It is hard for those thrust into extreme disgrace, desolation, poverty, and helplessness to believe in God's justice and goodness. . . . It is hard for the well-fed and the powerful to comprehend God's judgment and God's grace."[3]

We must take these words to heart. It is not that those who suffer from having too little, or who are spiritually deadened by having too much, have zero responsibility for their choices before God in Christ. But we must do what we can to prepare the way for them, rather than ignoring the very things that make receiving God's grace difficult for them. How do we do this? Bonhoeffer gives a concrete example: "If the hungry do not come to faith, the guilt falls on those who denied them bread."[4] We must feed the hungry. There is much to do. We must provide food and shelter, work for justice, and offer community. These are not requirements for people in need to become Christians. Bonhoeffer is careful to reject such a claim. But doing these things will prepare the way to the Way, removing obstacles to the reception of God's love and grace. Doing these things will help others discover and become followers of the Way.

The relationship between followers of Christ and those who do not share our faith is all too often strained, both in our personal lives and in the public square. Unfortunately, this is regularly due to a lack of humility and love on the part of Christians toward those who don't share our commitments. We should engage in good faith debate. Instead, we denigrate, deplore, and despise. Rather than seeking the common good via common ground, we dehumanize others by our words and deeds. We not only set obstacles between others and Christ by what we do and say; we *become* obstacles, making it more difficult for people to come to Christ. And many of us wrongly think that *others* are the problem, rather than we ourselves. We misinterpret and misapply the words of Jesus that the world will hate us because it hated him (John 15:18–21; Luke 6:22).

We are obligated to be preparers of the way. This requires repentance on our part. Humility is an essential component of repentance. In humility expressed through repentance, we admit our failures, our shortcomings, our self-centeredness, our callousness to sin and its impact on others. We turn to God and away from our sin.

Once we begin on the Way, Christ leads us into new ways of being good, new ways of being human. These new ways include love for God and neighbor, concrete love in action. We help others simply because they are human beings made in the image of God, people who have needs we can meet. We don't give someone food *so that* we can share the news of God's grace and forgiveness with them. Rather, we give them food because we love them, *and* we tell them about God's grace, if they are interested, because we love them. We don't hold them hostage by tethering their physical needs to listening to us. We simply serve them, doing what we can to meet their physical needs, and introduce them to Christ and his church, where their other needs can be met as well. We don't fight injustice and oppression *so that* we can share the gospel of forgiveness. We do so because justice is a part of the gospel of the kingdom of God. We seek to do it all in humility and love, just as Christ did and wants to do through his body, the church.

### Quit the Culture War

Many years ago, a professor of mine said that engaging ideas and people under the guise of a culture war is misguided. Christians, he said, should take a different approach. He was right. This was the late 1990s. I remember getting voting guides from the Christian Coalition as I walked into church one Sunday morning, with a list of issues that Christians should care about and where each candidate stood on those issues. Then, as now, people were claiming that to be a faithful Christian one must vote Republican (or Democrat).

When I was in college the "enemies" of the faith, according to many evangelicals, were relativism, liberalism, and Marxism. Over the years, the list grew. Postmodernism. Then the emergent church. Now it is critical race theory, wokeness, deconstruction, or progressive Christianity. Other Christian traditions have their lists, too. Christian nationalism is a current source of concern for many, and rightly so. Claims are still made about whom faithful Christians must vote for (both Republican and Democrat, depending on who is making the claim). And while character no longer appears to be a concern for many, the culture-war paradigm is alive and well. With the advent of social media and the explosion of other forms of partisan media outlets, the culture war has intensified. Many are weary of the culture-war approach. Others with large platforms, or who are seeking them, are digging their heels deeper into this miry clay because there are audiences to be had and dollars to be made. But the kingdom of God is not about audiences or dollars. It is about righteousness, justice, mercy, and truth.

By the time you are reading these words, it's likely that something new will be on the list. Rather than addressing particular issues, let's take a step back and ex-

amine the paradigm of the culture war and how it fails
to embody the righteousness, justice, and peace of the
kingdom of God. A crucial failure of the culture-war approach is that it leads us to see other people as enemies,
not fellow human beings made in God's image. When we
fall prey to this, all sorts of problems emerge.

In the culture war, we caricature others, their experiences, and their beliefs. We fail to understand, and perhaps fail to even try to understand, where they are coming from. This is because we are seeking to defeat them,
rather than relate to them in humility and love. Consider
what one megachurch pastor said about deconstruction
of one's Christian faith:

> You and I are in a day and age where deconstruction
> and the turning away from and leaving the faith has
> become some sort of sexy thing to do. I contend that
> if you ever experience the grace and mercy of Jesus
> Christ, actually—that that's really impossible to de-
> construct from. But if all you ever understand Chris-
> tianity to be is a moral code, then I totally get it. And
> if you find yourself in that spot, I'm telling you, I love
> you right now and we'll sit down with you and you
> don't have to punt on this thing. You might not have
> ever tried it. . . . To receive the mercy of God in your
> soul is to be forever changed.[5]

To his credit, this pastor expresses love and a willingness to talk with someone who is deconstructing or
is thinking about doing so. But notice the assumptions
and the not-so-subtle implied criticisms. People who de-

construct are following a "sexy" cultural trend. They see Christianity to be merely a moral code. And they were never actually genuine Christians to begin with, having never really been forever changed. Would you want to talk with this person, if you were deconstructing or thinking about doing so? Not likely. I'd actually advise against it.

While many of us are horrible at nuance, nuance is exactly what is needed in this and many similar discussions. Some do think of deconstruction as leaving the faith entirely. But that is not necessary, as the term can also refer to a close examination of assumptions and beliefs, seeking to remove those that are a product of culture instead of Christ. This kind of deconstruction can be healthy for one's faith.

Even more than nuance, we need humility and love. Whatever one's experience with deconstruction is, we are called to engage others in humility and love. This includes the person who leaves the faith for another faith, for agnosticism, or for atheism. It includes the Southern Baptist who becomes an Episcopalian, or the nondenominational evangelical who converts to Eastern Orthodoxy. It also includes the Christian who is trying to separate out the ways Christianity in America has become enmeshed with politics, assuming "true Christians" are Republicans or Democrats. It includes the process of examining the beliefs one has about the Bible and what it teaches, in order to understand which ones hold up to scrutiny and which do not. My point is not to defend or criticize anything related to these particular issues. Rather, it is to say that when we think of deconstruction as yet one more part of the culture war, it tends to produce failures of humility and love as we relate to those who have deconstructed or are in the process of doing so. This is not the Way.

Many disagree and continue to embrace the culture-war approach. One pastor and author has argued that we need a new strategy for winning the culture war: namely, have more children. He concludes that "the future belongs to the fecund. It's time for happy warriors who seek to 'renew the city' and 'win the culture war' by investing in their local church, focusing on the family, and bringing the kingdom to bear on the world, one baby at a time."[6] The notion that we should have children in order to win a culture war really troubles me. I resonate with some of what he argues for prior to this conclusion. There are better ways to foster Christian virtue and preserve orthodoxy than politics, politicians, or Supreme Court justices. It is vital that we disciple and catechize our children by our words and deeds. But I reject the notion that we should "have more children and disciple them" *as a strategy for winning the culture war*. We should have children because we believe God has called us to do so. But we should embrace the mystery of the child, love the children we are blessed to have, and do what we can to help them see and live out the goodness of God revealed in Jesus Christ.[7] We do this because our children are made in God's image and have intrinsic dignity as human beings, not to win a culture war. Having children in order to win a culture war is, simply put, wrong. It treats them as a means to some end, rather than an end in themselves. It misconstrues how followers of Christ should relate to the culture in which they live.

We shouldn't be concerned about winning a culture war. We shouldn't participate in a culture war or relate to others with a culture-war mindset. We should be concerned about manifesting the kingdom of God in humility and love, in righteousness, peace, and joy (Rom. 14:17) and in ways that manifest the fruit of the Spirit (Gal. 5:22–23). The culture-war paradigm goes astray from the Way because it creates an us-against-them approach that fails to reflect the nature and goodness of God and his kingdom. I'm not claiming that there are no battles to fight; that we have no enemies (otherwise we couldn't love our enemies as Jesus commands); that we should abandon politics, education, journalism, entertainment, or other culture-forming institutions. I am claiming that we should engage the world in all of these realms in ways that reflect humble love, rather than the belligerent and arrogant spirit so often present in Christians who adopt the culture-war paradigm.

We are called to live at peace with others, as far as it depends on us (Rom. 12:18). Certainly conflict is unavoidable, but culture warriors often neglect the serious call to seek peace and pursue it (1 Pet. 3:11). New Testament scholar Esau McCaulley helps us see an important connection here, the connection between peacemaking and justice.[8] He argues that peacemaking works together with truth telling; they should not be separated. As we seek to make peace on the way to a more just society, the truth must be told. We must tell the truth about racial injustice, about the objectification and commodification of black female bodies, about inequality in criminal sentencing, and much more. As we engage in peacemaking in this and other contexts, we are showing people what Christ and his kingdom are like. In this way, peacemaking is evangelistic. This means that the work of justice, which inherently includes peacemaking and truth telling, is evangelistic. It is one aspect of God's redemption of all creation. When we do this, we help prepare the way for people to know Christ and enter into his kingdom.

But so many Christians resist this. We insult. We attack. We want rhetorical victory more than redemption. When we see things through a culture-war lens, we are inclined to dig our heels in, rather than walk alongside each other in compassion, curiosity, humility, and love. For example, rather than taking an honest look at racial injustice and potential solutions, some Christians prefer to decry Black Lives Matter and focus on denouncing critical race theory. But we are mistaken if we choose to demonize Black Lives Matter and minimize, ignore, and in some cases excuse or even justify the suffering and death that led to its formation. We are mistaken if we focus on whatever philosophical flaws there might be in critical race theory while minimizing or even ignoring the injustices and suffering that it analyzes. We are wrong to focus more on protecting the alleged interests of institutions and their leaders than on the actual welfare and cries for justice of those who suffer from oppression or abuse.

Christians across the political spectrum have wrongly adopted this way of thinking and talking. There are examples on both sides of the political divide. Like some conservatives, some progressives evince a lack of forgiveness and charity. They are also guilty of dehumanizing their political opponents: calling them "deplorables," "Nazis," "snowflakes" (appropriating what was originally a conservative insult of progressives), and worse. Humility and love counsel us to act differently. We should quit the culture war and humbly seek the good of all with the transformative love of Christ.

We should also quit the culture war because its fruit is so often rotten. The dehumanizing and degrading rhetoric it produces is putrid. The damage done to human bodies and souls left in its wake is grim. Many have left the faith altogether because of the culture-war Christianity they experienced. Thankfully, many have come to see the differences between the Jesus of the Gospels and the counterfeit culture-warrior version of Jesus propagated by many. Many want to join with those who follow the authentic Jesus of the Gospels, the Jesus who came to serve and give his life for us, not the manufactured Jesus who wants to help take America back for God.

The Way of Christ is very different from the way of the culture war. As a friend of mine says, Christians should be working toward not a Christian state but a just state. Culture warriors tend to focus on advancing the self-interest of those who are part of their camp. Yet the Way of Christ is about humbly putting the interests of others before our own. Christian culture warriors often seek the consolidation of power to maintain privilege. But the Way of Christ is about sacrifice, sometimes giving up power, and centering our lives on God, his kingdom, and the well-being of all. "Christians of all people should not first be looking how to promote their own social subgroup or to promote only the welfare of other Christians, but should first be seeking how to address the common good."[9] It is Jesus, after all, who said that "the last will be first, and the first will be last" (Matt. 20:16).

If the culture-war approach is morally and spiritually bankrupt, what should we do in order to have a positive influence in our culture? How can we partner with God and others so that more of his kingdom comes, and more of his will is done, on earth as it is in heaven? There is so much to be done, and so much good work that is being done. A couple of examples will be helpful.

First, I'll offer one from my own experience. The three years I spent at Talbot School of Theology's graduate philosophy program were some of the most significant and formative times of my life, not just as a philosopher, but as a follower of Jesus, friend, husband, and father. The goal of the program is not to produce graduates who will use their education to Christianize our country or fight a culture war. Rather, it is to produce graduates who go on to work in academia, full-time ministry, law, business, education, and other professions who can demonstrate the plausibility of the Christian faith within the marketplace of ideas. Graduates are able to offer a Christian perspective in these different realms of society, showing the truth, goodness, and beauty of that perspective. Ideally, they are able to embody it, too. This is an important distinction. One approach focuses on the use of power, whereas the other focuses on rational persuasion and relational depth. One uses coercion and control, whereas the other evinces respect for all as creatures made in God's image.

As a second example, consider The Center for Christianity and Public Life. Founded in 2022, the center "is a new, nonpartisan institution in the nation's capital with the mission to contend for the credibility of Christian resources in public life, for the public good. We offer what we have not as an act of imposition, but out of a spirit of loving service."[10] The center is grounded in the conviction that character matters for leaders in all areas of society, including politics. Solid character, deep spiritual formation, and a commitment to service are central to its approach and mission.[11] This is exactly the kind of thing we need: a commitment to character, rather than ignoring it for political expediency; making spiritual formation central, rather than ignoring what our public life is doing to our hearts and the hearts of others. We need more people committed to all forms of public service in the Spirit of Christ, rather than seeking dominion over others in the spirit of our age.

Quitting the culture war doesn't mean Christians shouldn't engage the culture, including challenging views present or prevalent within it. Rather, it means that we do so from a posture of humility and love. Sometimes this will call for boldness. At other times, a patient gentleness will be the order of the day. We need each other, and the wisdom of the Spirit, to show us what is needed in our own lives and circumstances. But we should not see ourselves as culture warriors. Rather, we should see ourselves as humble servants seeking the good of all. As an old acquaintance of mine puts it, Jesus picks up a towel to serve, not a sword to slay, even washing the feet of his betrayer. We are to do the same as we engage people in our culture. We must stop attacking others in words and deeds. We must choose the way of the towel, not the way of the sword.[12] In this way, we walk in the steps of Jesus, the humble and loving servant of all.

### Preventing Polarization

Polarization is both fuel for and a fruit of the culture war. It's a common observation that our society has become increasingly polarized in recent years. There are at least three types of polarization in the United States: (1) ideological polarization; (2) affective polarization; and (3) attitude polarization.[13]

*Ideological polarization* refers to our beliefs about moral, social, religious, and political issues being consistently conservative or progressive. For example, in the political realm, the proportion of people with consistently liberal or consistently conservative positions *more than doubled* between 1994 and 2014. Many seem to think that political beliefs are like a package deal. You have to accept *all* of a party's platform to be a true member of that party.

*Affective polarization* has to do with how our views of and feelings toward people of the opposing party are increasingly negative (e.g., "Demonrats," "Repugs"). Those with a "very unfavorable" opinion of the opposing party *nearly tripled* between 1994 and 2016, and it's a safe bet that this increased during and subsequent to the Trump presidency. This leads us to think that people who have different views are not intelligent and are actually evil. We can't or won't see that they might have good reasons for what they believe or that their disagreement with us does not make them a bad Christian or a bad person.

Finally, *attitude polarization* describes how our disagreements have become increasingly sharp. In the 2020 election, some proclaimed, "If Biden wins, the US will become socialist and our country will collapse." Others worried that "if Trump wins, democracy as we know it will cease to exist and our country will become like the Handmaid's Tale." Consider presidential approval ratings, both historically and at present. The Republican/ Democrat presidential approval ratings averaged 75 percent Republican / 34 percent Democrat in the time of Nixon, 81 percent Republican / 23 percent Democrat in the time of George W. Bush, and, near the end of Trump's presidency, 95 percent Republican / 3 percent Democrat. In November of 2022, Biden was at 85 percent Democrat / 4 percent Republican.[14]

Sometimes there are good reasons to be polarized. Some beliefs and ideologies are false, evil, or harmful. I don't want to minimize the importance of deep and important religious, moral, and political convictions. But people of good heart and sound mind disagree on some issues, and we can't lose sight of this. What I want to focus on is how we handle disagreements, how we can exemplify the character of Christ in a polarized environment. It's too easy to assume that strong reactions against what we say are because of the ideas we are articulating and defending, when they may be due to the moral or intellectual vices we are manifesting.

The problem of polarization is us—you and me. All too often, Christians reflect the way of the world, rather than the Way of Christ. Many causes are in play here. This is not always easy to discern. Care is required, and virtuous character is essential. We need to be willing to undergo personal change in order to hear one another. And we need to do so to reflect the Way of Christ in our culture. The ancient Roman poet Horace said that "to flee vice is the beginning of virtue." Given this, it will be helpful to examine a few vices that contribute to polarization. If we flee vainglory, anger, and sloth, and put on humility and love, we can help prevent polarization and its toxic effects in our homes, churches, and society.

Vainglory is "the excessive and disordered desire for recognition and approval from others."[15] It is perfectly fine to want some recognition and approval for the good things that we've done and the goodness that we embody. Vainglory arises when we want too much recognition or are too concerned about what others think of us and our accomplishments. When our desire for praise, approval, or recognition from others is strong or even dominates our lives, vainglory has taken root in us.

Vainglory contributes to polarization in many ways: I don't admit that I'm wrong; I don't change my mind; if I'm being made to look bad or wrong, I strike back at others to save face. These days, polarizing words and deeds can help us get attention and the glory we misguidedly seek for ourselves. But why seek attention and glory? And what is the cost to our souls and the souls of others?

Instead of the vice of vainglory, we need the virtue of humility. In humility we grasp our own flaws and limitations. Humility disposes us to put the interests of others ahead of our own. Humility is part of the antidote to vainglory because, with this virtue, we remove ourselves from the center of our lives and value others and their interests much more highly. We are willing to sacrifice for them and their well-being. We don't try to get glory for ourselves. We are happy for others to receive it and for our lives to reflect the goodness, truth, beauty, and unity of God. In humility, we see people as fellow image bearers of God. That's the most significant fact about other people. Not that they are conservative, progressive, deconstructed, gay, or whatever. Humility gets us past polarization in a way that helps us engage others with the love of Christ.

Love has a key role to play here as well. There are many obstacles to love, but we'll focus on the vice of sloth. As we saw in chapter 3, sloth is resistance to the transformational demands of love. When I manifest sloth, I am indifferent to the needs of others and my obligations to them. Being responsive to these needs and obligations requires change, but sloth makes me resistant to that change.

We are to love God with all that we have—heart, soul, mind, and strength. Doing so requires commitment, sacrifice, time, effort, and dependence upon the Holy Spirit if we are to manifest love for God, his people, and the world. Rather than loving God with our minds, sloth may lead us to avoid a problem with our position that we ought to address but think others may not see. Polarizing speech can be a way to mask our ignorance and insecurity. It can also be the fruit of a slothful hatred of others. Sloth may also manifest itself as we use arguments and ideas to avoid communicating with others at a deeper and more emotionally intimate level. This is a way we may resist the demands of love.

Sloth might lead us to avoid engaging with others at all on controversial issues or to the busyness of trying to win every argument. This kind of busyness fosters polarization. Instead, we should slow down, take a breath, and try to figure out what love requires in each specific situation. I've erred in both ways over the years.

Anger also contributes to polarization. It seems to be the norm in our civil discourse about politics, theological disagreements, and ethical issues such as abortion, gun violence, and the pandemic and our differing responses to them. While there is such a thing as righteous anger, a lot, maybe even most, of our anger is unrighteous. It is self-centered, a fruit of not getting what we want rather than of our passion for God and his kingdom. Anger is an emotional response to not getting our way that includes a desire or decision to harm other people.[16] The harm can come through our words or actions. Such anger hurts others, divides churches, and hinders work for God's kingdom. It creates anything from hurt feelings to war or genocide. Anger also hurts us. It can fragment the soul of the person in its grip.

We are often angry in response to disagreement, which causes more polarization: "The sense of self-righteousness that comes with our anger simply provokes more anger and self-righteousness on the other side."[17] We need to stop this vicious cycle. Love is crucial for this. We must remember that there is a story behind every person's beliefs, words, and behavior. Often it is a story that includes significant suffering. We would do well to keep this in mind! It helps us avoid dehumanizing those we disagree with and understand them and where they are coming from, all of which undermines polarization. The practice of rhetorical nonviolence, discussed in chapter 4, can help us grow in humility and love and turn down the heat when discussing controversial issues in our polarized times.

Instead of sloth and anger, we need love. As we've seen, love is a disposition to will the good of others, to do what I can to promote what is good for them. We love someone when we promote that person's good for their sake. In this, we affirm that it is good that this person exists. If we love our neighbor as ourselves, if we grow into having a heart that really does will the good of others, including our enemies, and if we are making progress in loving God with all our heart, soul, mind, and strength, then we'll be able to talk with others in love about ideas that matter. This means that I see those I disagree with as people to love, rather than enemies to defeat, shame, mock, or hate. I approach them with humility rather than hubris. I see them as having worth and dignity, even in the midst of strong disagreement. This will help me engage as and when I should.

If we start from a place of humble love, we'll generate a lot more light in our discussions of difficult issues, rather than the heat that is created so often these days. Light leads people to the Way of Christ; heat often pushes them away. More importantly, light of this sort exemplifies the Way of Christ in the midst of a polarized culture. As George Marsden exhorts us, "Christians ought to be among those who are working the hardest to find common ground."[18] Let's do more of that. Find it. Build on it. Work alongside those who care about the common good. Let's bring more light into the world. Together.

## Pro-Life for All of Life

Many Christians contend that the gospel of personal salvation and transformation is the only solution to the injustices in our world. The idea is that if society is to change for the better, then the hearts of the individuals who make up that society must be changed. Widespread conversion to Christ is the only solution to the evils of racial injustice, gender discrimination, and gun violence, according to many. This can be part of the solution, given the transformation possible as one grows in Christ and connects with others in the church. Yet more than personal conversion is needed. Much more. Many Christians, including pastors, supported slavery in the United States and used the Bible to do so. Large segments of the church in Germany supported Hitler and the Nazis. Our faith is not individualistic; it is communal. It has social ramifications. We should not merely rely on personal salvation to solve interpersonal evil.

Interestingly, many who claim that the only way to make the world better is hearts being changed by the gospel also support using the force of law to make abortion illegal in the United States. Many who are pro-life address the trauma and deaths that are caused by racism, misogyny, gun violence, and war by relying solely on conversion and a change of heart, yet they change their tune when it comes to abortion. Many who are pro-choice want the government to stay out of the choice to abort or not but are willing to bring the law to bear on other types of choices we make. Changing laws will not resolve all of these issues. But what we are willing to use coercive legal force to accomplish is revealing, wherever we are on the political spectrum. We need principled reasons for when the force of law should be used and when it should not.

In the midst of culture-war rhetoric about baby-killers and social media posts with memes from *The Handmaid's Tale*, Bonhoeffer is once again helpful. He considers the different motives a woman might have for making such a choice, pointing out that she may choose to abort as "a deed of despair from the depths of human desolation or financial need, in which case guilt falls often more on the community than on the individual."[19] I think this is right. Moreover, in a society with less human desolation and financial need and more community and generous compassion, there would be a lot fewer abortions, regardless of the law. Many of the reasons women give as the primary ones for why they choose to abort reflect Bonhoeffer's insight here. Historical data show that the top two most frequent reasons for having an abortion are (1) the ways giving birth would interfere with education, work, or caring for dependents (74 percent); and (2) not being able to afford having a child (73 percent).[20] It is clear that better social support—including affordable child and elder care as well as better access to education and jobs that pay a living wage—would reduce the number of abortions in the United States.

As I write these words today, the Supreme Court's decision to overturn both *Roe* and *Casey* was announced. I am pro-life, in a particular sense, due to philosophical arguments related to the personhood and rights of the unborn. But I'm not sure how to best reflect that conviction in the law, given my agreement with Bonhoeffer on the guilt of the community for many of the abortions that occur, and given the fact that some abortions are morally justified. I think some legal restrictions on abortion are appropriate, but here I'm more concerned with the moral, spiritual, and interpersonal dimensions of this issue. The law should protect the most vulnerable among us, and the unborn are among the most vulnerable. But the law, society as a whole, and the church should also protect the vulnerable women and girls who are considering whether or not to abort a pregnancy. Christians differ about abortion. You don't have to be pro-life (or pro-choice) to be a follower of the Way. But those followers of the Way who are pro-life must be pro-life for all of human life. Let's consider why.[21]

Pro-life activist Scott Klusendorf defends the singular focus of the pro-life movement:

> abortion-choice advocates may insist that if pro-life advocates were truly "pro-life," they'd be "whole-life" and take on other "life" issues like poverty, immigration reform, support for refugees, foster care advocacy, better wages for the poor, gun control, and the

list goes on and on. However, most pro-lifers (so the argument goes) don't really care about these other issues. Thus, they are not "pro-life," only "pro-birth" or "anti-abortion." This, too, is unfair. Why should anyone believe that because you oppose the intentional killing of an innocent human being, you must therefore take responsibility for all societal ills? Pro-life advocates, as individuals, will care about many issues, not just a few. However, it does not follow that the operational objectives of the pro-life movement must be broad and inclusive as well.[22]

In one sense, Klusendorf is right. Being involved in the pro-life movement and focusing on abortion does not mean one must also give time and energy to every other societal ill. But that's not really the problem. The problem is that the pro-life movement must apply its beliefs to more than just abortion and should welcome a broader application of the term "pro-life."

Why?

Our theology of human beings should shape our understanding of what it means to be pro-life. Moral integrity and intellectual consistency require it. And embracing a pro-life ethic for all of life reflects the kingdom of God and respect for all human life. Sadly, some who are pro-life about abortion fail to consistently apply their beliefs to other life issues. They exemplify a callousness toward the well-being of immigrants, the continued suffering of racial and ethnic minorities in America, the avoidable deaths of innocent civilians due to American military actions, the tens of thousands of gun deaths that happen annually, and the morally unjust application of capital punishment in the United States. This leads to criticisms of the movement that have merit because when people advocate for the rights of the unborn, but are calloused, apathetic, or even opposed to the rights of other human beings made in God's image, they are guilty of hypocrisy. We must remember that "the pro-life position . . . is an inclusive view. It says no human being—regardless of size, skin color, level of development, race, gender, or place of residence—should be excluded from the community of human persons."[23] Not only must we remember it; we must live it.

The primary reason for adopting a whole life ethic is the Christian view that all human beings are made in the image of God. Our value is not found in what we can *do*, our economic, physical, intellectual, or even spiritual potential. Rather, it is grounded in what we *are*, image bearers of God. This is an inalienable aspect of our being. Even the most morally depraved among us retains this basic dignity.[24] And none of the following undermines that dignity: being unborn, immigration status, wealth, race, ethnicity, religion, sexual orientation, gender, or any other classification that humans use to marginalize one another and justify maltreatment.

In 2017, 862,000 abortions were performed in the United States. Fifty-nine percent of women who have abortions have had at least one birth, and 24 percent of women in the United States will have an abortion by the time they are forty-five.[25] For those who are pro-life, these numbers are alarming. Yet every single human being is made in God's image, not just the unborn. There are many other life issues in the United States. For example, in 2020 over 45,000 people died due to gun violence in America. Or consider the death penalty. Set aside whether or not it is in principle consistent with a Christian ethic. In practice, it certainly is not. Since 1973, 185 death-row inmates have been exonerated, while others have had their capital offenses cleared. Still more have been posthumously exonerated. We don't know how many of the 1,547 people who have been executed since 1976 were innocent, but many likely were.[26] In addition, there is a clear bias against defendants of color and in favor of white victims.[27] Statistically, police officers are more aggressive in encounters with black Americans, which can lead to all sorts of trauma, injury, and death.[28] Finally, consider the horrific things that have been done to human beings at our southern border. Children died after being denied entry into the country.[29] Others died in custody.[30] The fate of many more is unknown. Our government used Covid-19 as an excuse to send thousands of migrant children back to their countries of origin.[31] But it's worse than that. We screened them, and many who tested negative for the virus were then sent back under the pretext that they had it, rather than following immigration law and placing them in the custody of the Department of Health and Human Services to find sponsors for them until a hearing. Other atrocities at the border detention facilities and present in our immigration processes have been widely reported.[32] The suffering, trauma, and death caused by wars across the planet are beyond what we can even comprehend, and much of it happens with the support of "pro-life" Christians in America.

This leads us to a central reason in support of a more expansive pro-life movement: the need to display ethical integrity and intellectual consistency. I understand the passion of many abortion opponents and the conviction that abortion is *the* moral issue of our time. But the movement, as I once heard Robert George say when he visited the university where I teach, must have integrity. It must be trustworthy. George was explaining why he was against the actions of some in the pro-life movement who recorded videos of Planned Parenthood employees under false pretenses.[33] I wholeheartedly agree with him that the pro-life movement must be above reproach. People must be able to rely on the data, evidence, and arguments that it provides. And they must believe that those in the movement, especially its leaders, are trustworthy people with sound moral character and rigorous intellectual consistency. I am sad to say that my own interactions with some in the movement have revealed serious flaws on both counts.

For those who are pro-life, two things must be kept in mind. First, "all the great movements for social justice in our society have strongly emphasized a love ethic."[34] If we advocate for the unborn but show disdain for the women who face agonizingly difficult reproductive choices, it doesn't matter what the law is. Without love, we will have failed. Second, we must keep in mind that "there can be no love without justice."[35] Many in the pro-life camp focus on what justice requires for the unborn. But what does justice require for the pregnant child who is a victim of rape? What does justice require for the woman who can barely make ends meet as it is, who is pregnant and not sure how she will feed and care for herself and her children? We must ask these questions and wrestle with the possible answers. It seems to me that for some, being pro-life really does just mean being pro-birth. This is not the Way.

Not everyone who has pro-life convictions must be involved in all of these causes, or at least involved in all of them to the same degree. This is part of what it means to be a member of the body of Christ. We all have different callings and roles to play. Some primarily focus on abortion, others on immigration, racism, or something else, as led by their convictions and the Spirit. But we must not ignore or downplay the fact that the very theological and moral truths that undergird the pro-life abortion position also apply to other life issues. To do so is a failure of humility before the truth and other people. It is also a failure of love for those who desperately need it. Moreover, advocating for the pro-life cause in abortion while minimizing or opposing its implications for racial justice, immigration, or gun violence is an intellectual, moral, and spiritual failure. We must affirm the truth that all human beings are made in God's image and then let that truth guide us in our words and deeds. This is the way of humility and love. This is the Way of Christ.

Finally, consider a question, one that is crucial not only for the effectiveness but more importantly for the faithfulness of the pro-life movement: If we want to cultivate a culture that values *all* human life, why would we *not* want to expand the pro-life vision? If pro-life Christians across the political and theological spectrum were known for being pro-life for all of life, there would of course be opposition, but at least we would embody intellectual and moral integrity, rather than what looks like political partisanship or outright hypocrisy, both of which are obstacles to the Way.

## Conclusion

Many other things can be obstacles to faith. A bad religious upbringing, traumatic experiences in church, hypocrisy and other sin in the church, disappointment with God, and hard questions can hinder faith. For others, it might be Christian nationalism, militarism, or the ways many in the church serve the powers of this world. We serve God and others by doing what we can to remove these and other obstacles, in humility and love, to prepare the way for them to become followers of the Way, if they so choose.

Unfortunately, it is too often the case that the face we are showing the world is nothing like the face of Christ. Instead of humility and love, we show anger, hatred, and sloth. But there is a better way.

In 2006, a man entered a small Amish school in a small Pennsylvania town, gunning down five children before taking his own life with that same gun.[36] I cannot imagine the anger, rage, and despair that one would feel in the face of such an avoidable tragedy, as a parent and member of the community. But the immediate reaction of the leaders in this Amish community was, in many ways, shocking. Their response to the shooting was to go to the widow of the shooter, offer forgiveness, and ask that she remain a part of their community. A father of one of the murdered children explained, "That is how God puts his word into the world." Indeed. Forgiveness is a way to put God's word in the world. This is also true of humble love—it is another way God puts his word into the world. If we want to play a part in preparing the way for others to become followers of the Way, putting God's word into the world by manifesting humility and love is an excellent place to begin.

six

# *Persevering on the Way*

I've cultivated a Spotify playlist that I regularly add songs to entitled "Memento Mori," a Latin phrase meaning "Remember that you will die." Sounds like a fun list of songs, right?[1] (I also have one entitled "Memento Vivere," which means "Remember to live." My music isn't all doom and gloom.) The songs on my Memento Mori playlist remind me not only of the transitoriness of life but also of its beauty and goodness. The wise, insightful, and sometimes poignant expressions of truths about life and death from Johnny Cash, The Red Hot Chili Peppers, REM, The Lost Dogs, The Steeldrivers, Bruce Springsteen, NEEDTOBREATHE, and others touch something deep in my soul.

I've included several songs from U2, whose songs have reverberated across the years of my life since my high school days like no other band. Multiple layers of meaning are present in one of my favorite songs on this playlist, "Walk On," as in many of their songs. Bono has said all of their songs can be interpreted at one level as a kind of prayer. "Walk On" fits the bill here, as a prayerful encouragement to persevere through life's difficulties. Even when the light seems far off and we're tempted to turn back, we keep going:

> And I know it aches
> And your heart it breaks
> And you can only take so much.
> Walk on, walk on.

On the *Elevation* tour, the band would often use this song to close out the night. When they played it, there would be a large projection of a suitcase with a heart inside it, the image scrolling up the wall, "filling up the dark spaces between stage and ceiling and highlighting the theme of love's eternal and transcendent nature."[2] The song begins with words about love: "And love is not the easy thing; The only baggage you can bring; Is all that you can't leave behind." Bono explains the importance of love in the context of both the song and life:

> Love, in the highest sense of the word, is the only thing that you can always take with you, in your heart. At some point you are going to have to lose everything else anyway. There's a passage in Corinthians that uses the image of a house going through a fire, and it seems to suggest that when, in death, we eventually face judgment (or inspection, as one translation puts it) all that is made of straw and wood will be burned away, only the eternal things will survive. . . . Whatever it is that you want more than love, it has to

go. That's a really interesting question to ask: What
are the things you want more than love?[3]

An interesting question, indeed, one that matters a
lot in the song and in life. Sometimes, however, it is not
the things we want more than love that make it "not the
easy thing." Rather, it is the struggles, the trials, and the
adversity we face in this life. The song addresses this as
well. It encourages us to persevere, to keep going even if
we do, for a time, give up. But this is not a shallow, feel-
good piety that ignores the darkness and pain. The song
realistically addresses life's suffering and our longing for
change, as we "can only take so much."

We can take only so much. But we are given so much,
too, if we would only humbly receive it. We can only take
so much, but we can also take love with us, leaving behind much of what we build, make, and break, as the
song concludes. It takes humility to accept this, to come
to grips with the triviality and transitoriness of much of
what we chase after in life. It takes humility to recognize
that something matters more than our achievements,
more than comfort, more than getting the things we often want more than love. But the beautifully simple yet
profound message of "Walk On" is that we need a heart
full of love to persevere in this life, and we take that heart
full of love with us into the next one. We need humility
and love to persevere on the Way. It's not only Bono who
tells us this; it's also the Bible. I suspect the Bible played a
part in U2's inspiration for this song, as it often does.

As I mentioned above, I use this song and the playlist
as a way to practice the spiritual discipline of memento

mori, the discipline of thinking about the reality of our death. Marlena Graves describes the different ways this remembrance of death has been practiced by Christians since ancient times.[4] Keeping a marble skull on one's desk, installing a coffin in one's bedroom (I'll pass on that one), and placing artwork in churches depicting people dancing with skeletons are just a few of the concrete ways Christians have reminded themselves of death's reality. Spending time with the sick or dying, while done out of love for them, can also remind us of life's brevity and death's reality. I've learned a lot about this from my wife, a hospice nurse serving the dying and their families in humility and love.

Aging itself can be incorporated into the practice of memento mori. When I was in my late forties, a fellow Christian philosopher told me that after turning fifty he thought about death a lot more. I thought it was funny at the time. Now that I'm in my early fifties I've had the same experience. Sometimes when I reflect on my death, I fear the possibility that I'll just completely go out of existence. That thought of utter nonexistence sometimes brings a deep and cold fear to my soul. But I really do believe that God is love and that Jesus rose from the dead. I really do. This anchors my hope in my own resurrection, the resurrection of others, and the restoration of all things in Christ.

The point of this practice is not to think morosely about death. Memento mori attunes us to the everyday moments of joy we all too often miss. It also helps us align our priorities with the priorities of God and his kingdom. This is important because life here is short, and many things can lead us astray. Life doesn't always *seem* short, however. Trials, suffering, and adversity can make the days and nights seem long. Sometimes very long. The practice of memento mori is so helpful as we seek to persevere on the Way in the midst of both the joys and the sorrows.

But what is perseverance? It is "an ability not to be derailed from one's purpose by adversity."[5] The phrase Eugene Peterson borrowed from Nietzsche comes to mind when I think of perseverance: a long obedience in the same direction. Such obedience is not just about what we do; it also applies to who we are. We need it to persevere in humility and love as people of the Way.

As followers of the Way, marked by the humility and love of Christ, we must face adversity in ways that foster our growth as little Christs. The Scriptures make the connection between character and adversity clear: "Consider it pure joy, my brothers and sisters, whenever you face trials of many kinds, because you know that the testing of your faith produces perseverance. Let perseverance finish its work so that you may be mature and complete, not lacking anything" (James 1:2–4 NIV). I often face trials in survival mode instead of pure joy mode. In moments of total honesty with God, I've told him that I would prefer he end the trial in question, even if that means less character growth for me. But at other moments, better moments, I accept the reality of the trial and decide I don't want to waste it. So I persevere. Why?

For one thing, the trial drives me toward God and away from my sometimes apathetic comfort. I also persevere because of the ways doing so brings the maturity

James writes about, the development of character and a deeper grasp of the love of God. These fruits of perseverance are also described in Romans 5:3–5: "We also glory in our sufferings, because we know that suffering produces perseverance; perseverance, character; and character, hope. And hope does not put us to shame, because God's love has been poured out into our hearts through the Holy Spirit, who has been given to us" (NIV). Receiving God's love in new ways, becoming aware of it in new ways, is humbling. It also gives us a source of love to share with others. This growth in character that can result from suffering, anchored in hope, deepens our ability to persevere.

Another way to grow in our ability to persevere as followers of the Way is by persevering in the practices of the Way. I feel my failure here, often acutely. It can be a struggle sometimes for me to engage in spiritual practices. Spiritual formation and moral development are two of my primary areas of research, but I know more about these subjects from reading and thinking about them than I do from actually practicing them. I sometimes allow my perfectionistic tendencies and feelings of guilt to keep me from engaging in these practices, even though they are exactly what I need to open my heart and life up to God and his grace. When I am consistent, the good that results in my relationship with God and others and in the other dimensions of my life makes me wonder why I sometimes lack that consistency.

We can be too idealistic. We can think that for a practice to be valuable we need to have some deep experience in the moment, learn some profound new truth, or gain a new insight about ourselves. Yet sometimes God might just want to remind us of something we already know; or perhaps the apparent fruitlessness of the practice on any given day is only apparent. Persevering in practices of the Way can be useful as simple ways to faithfully seek God. Nothing spectacular is required, just ordinary faithfulness.

We don't persevere in these practices for ourselves alone, but also for others. Persevering in the practices of the Way helps us to persevere as preparers of the way to the Way. Recall some of Bonhoeffer's insights from chapter 5. Being a preparer of the way for others so they are better able to become followers of the Way involves feeding the hungry, providing shelter for the unhoused, securing justice for all, and providing community for the lonely. But when we look at the world, the temptation to give in to despair and give up is strong. People are starving in the midst of great prosperity, others have no safe place to live and sleep, rights are routinely violated in ways that offend our basic humanity, and so many of the lonely remain alone. The battle seems lost, even though Christ reveals and the Scriptures proclaim that it is ultimately going to be won. Swords really will be made into plowshares. Violence will cease. A community of humility and love, where the needs of all are met, will become real in the new heavens and the new earth. All of creation will be redeemed. All will be set right again by the Creator.

Humility reminds us of our limits and helps us remain other-centered as we continue in our work as preparers of the way. Love moves us to continue to work at bringing God's kingdom to bear in this fallen world. Humility and love—in union with Christ and our local church, lived out in our communities and the wider world—move us and everything else in that Godward direction. Little by little, day by day, these virtues make us better fit for the kingdom coming in this life and the kingdom in its fullness in the next. The process will usually be slow, often happening in fits and starts. Bono describes this slowness of spiritual change well:

> Your nature is a hard thing to change; it takes time. . . . I have heard of people having life-changing, miraculous turn-arounds, people set free from addiction after a single prayer. . . . But it was not like that for me. For all that "I was lost, I am found," it is probably more accurate to say, "I was really lost, I'm a little less so at the moment." And then a little less and a little less again. That to me is the spiritual life. The slow reworking and rebooting of a computer at regular intervals, reading the small print of the service manual. It has slowly rebuilt me in a better image. It has taken years, though, and it is not over yet.[6]

It's hard to change. It takes time. If we experience a miraculous, instantaneous turnaround, we can be grateful. But we can also be grateful if we experience it over time, as we remain faithful, as God's presence and power transform us little by little, day by day, month by month, year by year, into little Christs. Whether it happens in an instant or in a few decades, this kind of change is miraculous.

One last U2 reference. Bono sings about this kind of change in another of my favorite songs, "Love and Peace or Else": "As you enter this life, I pray you depart, with a wrinkled face, and a brand new heart." This is my prayer for myself and for you. We come into the world with the wrinkled face of a newborn. We come into it with a relatively new physical heart, too, as we begin life outside of the womb and in the world. If God so blesses us, we exit this life with the wrinkled face of an old human being and an old physical heart. But hopefully we have a brand-new spiritual heart, transformed by our God at the core of our being in ways we may not dare to hope at present. But hope we can, and hope we must. We must not lose sight of the fact that God actually does make our hearts new again. We need not be held captive by pride, false humility, hatred, greed, or apathy. Instead, we can have a heart, and a life, infused with humility and love. We can have a heart, and a life, infused with the heart and life of Jesus.

In humility and love, as we rediscover the Way, we "take hold of the life that is truly life" (1 Tim. 6:19 NIV). But rediscovering the Way is not merely about what we believe. It is also about who we are and how we live. Thomas Merton reminds us of this important truth: "The spiritual life is first of all a *life*. It is not merely something to be known and studied, it is to be lived."[7] As we've explored persevering on the Way and reflected on some of the difficulties of remaining on that Way, we must not lose sight of this fact. We are not merely considering ideas, but the very substance of our lives as followers of Jesus.

We rediscover the Way when we center our lives on the humility and love of Christ as people of the Way. Engaging in practices of the Way nourishes our union with Christ and cultivates his character in us. As followers of the Way we seek to help others by preparing the way to the Way, embodying it in union with Christ and each other. We persevere in the Way when the virtues of humility and love are at the heart of our union with Christ and our relationships with others. As sojourners on the Way, we persevere; we hold fast and remain on the Way until our lives here end. Then the humility and love of Christ that we've seen through a glass darkly (1 Cor. 13:12) become real to us in ways we cannot imagine at present, as we see Jesus face-to-face for the first time.

We've lost humility and love as we've wandered from the tried-and-true Way of Christ. Humility and love are essential not only for rediscovering that Way but also for remaining on it and becoming people of it. These simple truths are not only to be believed. They must also be lived.

This is the Way.

# Next Steps

Growth in humility is a lifelong challenge, but as we've seen we can make real progress as followers of the Way. If you wish to continue your journey in understanding humility and want some practical ways to cultivate humility, here are some resources to check out:

Michael W. Austin and R. Douglas Geivett, eds., *Being Good: Christian Virtues for Everyday Life* (Eerdmans, 2012).

Richard Foster, *Learning Humility: A Year of Searching for a Vanishing Virtue* (IVP, 2022).

Marlena Graves, *The Way Up Is Down: Becoming Yourself by Forgetting Yourself* (IVP, 2020).

Kibeom Lee and Michael C. Ashton, *The H Factor of Personality* (Wilfrid Laurier University Press, 2012).

Andrew Murray, *Humility* (various editions).

Kathleen Norris, *The Quotidian Mysteries: Laundry, Liturgy, and "Women's Work"* (Paulist Press, 1998).

N. T. Wright, *Paul for Everyone: The Prison Letters; Ephesians, Philippians, Colossians, and Philemon* (Westminster John Knox, 2004).

For a growing list of resources, including practical steps for growth in humility, see:

https://michaelwaustin.com/cultivating-humility/

# Notes

**Chapter One**

1. See Acts 9:2; 19:9, 23; 22:4; 24:14, 22.

2. David H. Stern, *Jewish New Testament Commentary: A Companion Volume to the Jewish New Testament* (Clarksville, MD: Jewish New Testament Publications, 1992), 39, 107, 200–201.

3. "Modern Martyrs," Westminster Abbey, accessed March 22, 2021, https://www.westminster-abbey.org/about -the-abbey/history/modern-martyrs.

4. Rebecca Konyndyk DeYoung, *Glittering Vices: A New Look at the Seven Deadly Sins and Their Remedies*, 2nd ed. (Grand Rapids: Brazos, 2020), 15.

5. C. S. Lewis, *Mere Christianity* (San Francisco: Harper-One, 2015), 177.

6. Dallas Willard, *The Divine Conspiracy: Rediscovering Our Hidden Life in God* (San Francisco: Harper, 1998), 283–84.

7. Dallas Willard, *Renovation of the Heart: Putting on the Character of Christ* (Colorado Springs: NavPress, 2002), 15.

8. "Resolution on Moral Character of Public Officials— SBC.Net," accessed March 18, 2021, https://www.sbc.net/re

source-library/resolutions/resolution-on-moral-character
-of-public-officials/.

9. See Christian Miller, *The Character Gap: How Good Are We?* (New York: Oxford University Press, 2017), chs. 3–7.

10. "The End of Absolutes: America's New Moral Code," Barna Group, accessed March 30, 2021, https://www.barna .com/research/the-end-of-absolutes-americas-new-moral -code/.

11. Mark Galli, "Mastering the Golf Swing of Life," *Christianity Today*, June 28, 2012, http://www.christianitytoday .com/ct/2012/juneweb-only/golf-and-christian-ethics.html.

12. Aristotle, *Nicomachean Ethics*, trans. Terence Irwin, 2nd ed. (Indianapolis: Hackett, 1999), 19.

13. Dallas Willard, *Life without Lack: Living in the Fullness of Psalm 23* (Nashville: Thomas Nelson, 2018), 121.

14. Gravity Leadership Podcast, "Episode 9: The Goal of Discipleship Is Divine Union (Part 1)," accessed July 12, 2021, https://gravityleadership.com/podcast/goal-divine-union-1/.

15. Augustine, *The Trinity*, 2nd ed. (Hyde Park, NY: New City Press, 2012), 172.

16. Willard, *The Divine Conspiracy*, 276; emphasis in the original.

17. Marlena Graves, *The Way Up Is Down: Becoming Yourself by Forgetting Yourself* (Downers Grove, IL: IVP, 2020), 87.

18. Dietrich Bonhoeffer, *Life Together* (Minneapolis: Fortress, 2015).

## Chapter Two

1. Richard A. Burridge, *Imitating Jesus: An Inclusive Approach to New Testament Ethics* (Grand Rapids: Eerdmans, 2007), 232.

2. Much of what follows is drawn from my *Humility and Human Flourishing: A Study in Analytic Moral Theology* (Oxford: Oxford University Press, 2018), 28–38, 40–82.

3. Gordon D. Fee, *Paul's Letter to the Philippians* (Grand Rapids: Eerdmans, 1995), 50.

4. Ben Witherington III, *Paul's Letter to the Philippians: A Socio-Rhetorical Commentary* (Grand Rapids: Eerdmans, 2011), 120–21.

5. C. S. Lewis, *Mere Christianity* (San Francisco: HarperOne, 2015), 128.

6. Sister Joan Chittister, *Becoming Fully Human: The Greatest Glory of God* (Lanham, MD: Sheed & Ward, 2005), 115.

7. Dallas Willard, *The Allure of Gentleness: Defending the Faith in the Manner of Jesus* (New York: HarperOne, 2015), 115.

8. Richard B. Hays, *First Corinthians*, Interpretation: A Bible Commentary for Teaching and Preaching (Louisville: Westminster John Knox, 2011), 231.

9. Ben Witherington III, *Conflict and Community in Corinth: A Socio-Rhetorical Commentary on 1 and 2 Corinthians* (Grand Rapids: Eerdmans, 1995), 94–97.

10. Much of the interpretation that follows is drawn from Witherington, *Conflict and Community in Corinth*, 264–73.

11. Witherington, *Conflict and Community in Corinth*, 264.

12. Craig S. Keener, *1–2 Corinthians* (Cambridge: Cambridge University Press, 2005), 109.

13. For this and more on how chapter 13 is related to the rest of Paul's letter, see Hays, *First Corinthians*, 221–33.

14. Hays, *First Corinthians*, 227.

15. Hays, *First Corinthians*, 228.

16. Hays, *First Corinthians*, 231.

## Chapter Three

1. One biography of his life is Gordon C. Zahn, *In Solitary Witness: The Life and Death of Franz Jägerstätter* (Boston: Beacon, 1968). We have an account from Jägerstätter himself in a collection edited by Erna Putz, *Franz Jägerstätter: Letters and Writings from Prison*, trans. Robert A. Krieg (Maryknoll, NY: Orbis, 2009).

2. Zahn, *In Solitary Witness*, 13.

3. Zahn, *In Solitary Witness*, 15.

4. Quoted in Lawrence J. Danks, *Your Unfinished Life: The Classic and Timeless Guide to Finding Happiness and Success through Kindness* (n.p.: Helpful Media, 2009), 53.

5. Gregory, "On the Gospel (Homily 7)," accessed July 28, 2021, http://lectionarycentral.com/advent4/GregoryGreat.html.

6. Bonaventure, *Bonaventure: The Soul's Journey into God, The Tree of Life, The Life of St. Francis*, trans. Ewert Cousins (Mahwah, NJ: Paulist Press, 1978), 129.

7. Dietrich von Hildebrand, *Humility: Wellspring of Virtue* (Manchester, NH: Sophia Institute Press, 1997), 5.

8. John Cassian, *Institutes* 12.32, https://www.newadvent.org/fathers/350712.htm.

9. Teresa of Ávila, *Interior Castle or The Mansions*, trans. E. Allison Peers (Radford, VA: Wilder, 2008), 24.

10. Benedict, *The Rule of St. Benedict*, ed. Carolinne White (London: Penguin Classics, 2008).

11. John Climacus, *Ladder of Divine Ascent*, step 25, "On Humility," accessed July 28, 2021, https://www.fatheralexander.org/booklets/english/vainglory_ladder_climacus.htm#_Toc530064365.

12. Andrew Murray, *Humility: The Journey toward Holiness* (Minneapolis: Bethany House, 2001), 12.

13. Teresa of Ávila, *Interior Castle or The Mansions*, 143.

14. Thomas Merton, *Thoughts in Solitude* (New York: Farrar, Straus, and Giroux, 1958), 22.

15. Augustine, *On Christian Doctrine* 1.27; accessed December 13, 2021, https://www.newadvent.org/fathers/12021.htm.

16. bell hooks, *All about Love: New Visions* (New York: William Morrow, 2018), 14.

17. Augustine, *The Trinity* 4.1, ed. John E. Rotelle OSA, 2nd ed. (Hyde Park, NY: New City Press, 2012).

18. Teresa of Ávila, *The Way of Perfection* 16; accessed December 9, 2021, https://ccel.org/ccel/teresa/way/way.ii.html.

19. Paul K. Moser, *The Evidence for God: Religious Knowledge Reexamined*, updated edition (Cambridge: Cambridge University Press, 2009), 91.

20. Matthew W. Bates, *Salvation by Allegiance Alone: Rethinking Faith, Works, and the Gospel of Jesus the King* (Grand Rapids: Baker Academic, 2017), 77–100.

21. Josef Pieper, *The Four Cardinal Virtues*, trans. Richard Winston et al. (Notre Dame: University of Notre Dame Press, 1966), 6.

22. David G. Myers, "Humility: Psychology Meets Theology," *Reformed Review* 48 (1995): 195–206.

23. Pieper, *The Four Cardinal Virtues*, 22.

24. Joseph Butler, *Fifteen Sermons* (London: G. Bell and Sons, 1914), 83.

25. This account of justice is drawn from William C. Mattison III, *Introducing Moral Theology: True Happiness and the Virtues* (Grand Rapids: Brazos, 2008), 135–43.

26. This discussion of humility and pride is adapted from

my book *Humility and Human Flourishing: A Study in Analytic Moral Theology* (Oxford: Oxford University Press, 2018), 171–76.

27. C. S. Lewis, *Mere Christianity* (San Francisco: HarperOne, 2015), 121.

28. Lewis, *Mere Christianity*, 122.

29. Reinhold Niebuhr, *The Nature and Destiny of Man*, vol. 1 (Louisville: Westminster John Knox, 1996), 186–203.

30. See my article "Do I Drink Virtuously? A Christian Perspective," accessed July 5, 2022, https://www.equip.org/article/do-i-drink-virtuously-a-christian-perspective/.

31. Gisela H. Kreglinger, *The Spirituality of Wine* (Grand Rapids: Eerdmans, 2016).

32. Kreglinger, *The Spirituality of Wine*, 31. See Luke 7:34.

33. https://twitter.com/RepKinzinger/status/154432733 5830327301; accessed July 5, 2022.

34. Rebecca Konyndyk DeYoung, Colleen McCluskey, and Christina Van Dyke, *Aquinas's Ethics: Metaphysical Foundations, Moral Theory, and Theological Context* (Notre Dame: University of Notre Dame Press, 2009), 139.

35. R. Douglas Geivett, "Forgiveness," in *Being Good*, ed. Michael W. Austin and R. Douglas Geivett (Grand Rapids: Eerdmans, 2012), 204–41.

36. Rebecca Konyndyk DeYoung, "Courage," in Austin and Geivett, *Being Good*, 145–68.

37. DeYoung, "Courage," 147.

38. DeYoung, "Courage," 163.

39. DeYoung, "Courage," 164.

40. Rebecca Konyndyk DeYoung, *Glittering Vices: A New Look at the Seven Deadly Sins and Their Remedies*, 2nd ed. (Grand Rapids: Brazos, 2020), ch. 5.

41. Anne Lamott, *Operating Instructions: A Journal of My Son's First Year* (New York: Ballantine Books, 1994), 96.

42. DeYoung, *Glittering Vices*, 92.

43. Henri J. M. Nouwen, *The Return of the Prodigal Son: A Story of Homecoming* (New York: Doubleday, 1992), 106.

44. Nouwen, *The Return of the Prodigal Son*, 128–29.

45. Marlena Graves, *The Way Up Is Down: Becoming Yourself by Forgetting Yourself* (Downers Grove, IL: IVP, 2020), 10.

## Chapter Four

1. Dietrich Bonhoeffer, *Ethics* (Minneapolis: Fortress, 2015), 311.

2. It is difficult to know where to start, given the size of this literature. I would recommend starting with a more contemporary book or two, and then branching out into some of the historical authors discussed in that book. I'd suggest Richard J. Foster, *Celebration of Discipline* (San Francisco: HarperSanFrancisco, 1990); Marlena Graves, *The Way Up Is Down* (Downers Grove, IL: IVP, 2020); or Ruth Haley Barton, *Invitation to Solitude and Silence* (Downers Grove, IL: IVP, 2010). A great classic work to start with is *The Imitation of Christ* by Thomas à Kempis, trans. William Creasy (Macon, GA: Mercer University Press, 2015).

3. Dallas Willard, *The Spirit of the Disciplines: Understanding How God Changes Lives* (San Francisco: HarperSanFrancisco, 1988), 3–6.

4. Willard, *The Spirit of the Disciplines*, 5–6.

5. Dietrich Bonhoeffer, *Life Together* (Minneapolis: Fortress, 2015).

6. Bonhoeffer, *Life Together*, 10.

7. Bonhoeffer, *Life Together*, 13.

8. Bonhoeffer, *Life Together*, 3.

9. Katie Hays, *God Gets Everything God Wants* (Grand Rapids: Eerdmans, 2021), 131.

10. Bonhoeffer, *Life Together*, 5.

11. Bonhoeffer, *Life Together*, 6.

12. John Cassian, *Conference* 14.10, accessed July 19, 2022, https://ccel.org/ccel/cassian/conferences/conferences.iii.v.x.html.

13. Bonhoeffer, *Life Together*, 18.

14. Bonhoeffer, *Life Together*, 18.

15. Bonhoeffer, *Life Together*, 27; emphasis in the original.

16. Bonhoeffer, *Life Together*, 29–32.

17. Bonhoeffer, *Life Together*, 31–32.

18. C. René Padilla, *What Is Integral Mission?* (Minneapolis: Fortress, 2021), 42.

19. Bonhoeffer, *Life Together*, 57.

20. Bonhoeffer, *Life Together*, 57.

21. "Centering Prayer on the App Store," accessed July 19, 2022, https://apps.apple.com/us/app/centering-prayer/id844280857.

22. Bonhoeffer, *Life Together*, 59.

23. Willard, *The Spirit of the Disciplines*, 162; emphasis in the original.

24. See my book *Humility and Human Flourishing: A Study in Analytic Moral Theology* (Oxford: Oxford University Press, 2018), 187–88.

25. Willard, *The Spirit of the Disciplines*, 164–65.

26. Bonhoeffer, *Life Together*, 69–86.

27. Bonhoeffer, *Life Together*, 75.

28. Bonhoeffer, *Life Together*, 76.

29. Bonhoeffer, *Life Together*, 77.

30. Bonhoeffer, *Life Together*, 79.

31. Martin Luther King, "The Nobel Peace Prize 1964," NobelPrize.org, accessed June 28, 2022, https://www.nobel prize.org/prizes/peace/1964/king/acceptance-speech/.

32. Malcolm Foley, "The Gospel Has Never Been Colorblind," ChristianityToday.com, accessed June 23, 2022, https://www.christianitytoday.com/ct/2020/august-web -only/gospel-has-never-been-colorblind.html.

33. Malcolm Foley, "On Healing: Learning from Separatists," *Mere Orthodoxy*, May 2, 2022, https://mereorthodoxy .com/on-healing-learning-from-separatists/.

34. The Dietrich Bonhoeffer Institute, "COVID-19: Gun Violence Prevention, Ethics, and Theology, 2020," https:// www.youtube.com/watch?v=RDeqpGDZSpA.

35. Jemar Tisby, *The Color of Compromise: The Truth about the American Church's Complicity in Racism* (Grand Rapids: Zondervan, 2019), ch. 11.

36. Tisby, *The Color of Compromise*, 202.

37. Vincent Bacote, "Drawing from the Well: Learning from African American Christian Formation," in *Tending Soul, Mind, and Body: The Art and Science of Spiritual Formation*, ed. Gerald Hiestand and Todd Wilson (Downers Grove, IL: IVP Academic, 2019), 92–103.

38. This section draws on material in my article "Anger, Humility, and Civil Discourse," in *Righteous Indignation: Christian Philosophical and Theological Perspectives on Anger*, ed. Gregory L. Bock and Court D. Lewis (Lanham, MD: Fortress Academic, 2021), 115–24.

39. Kevin Dorst, "What Is Polarization?," *Reasonably Polarized*, September 18, 2020, https://www.psychologytoday.com /us/blog/reasonably-polarized/202009/what-is-polarization.

40. See my book *God and Guns in America* (Grand Rapids: Eerdmans, 2020).

41. Ronald J. Sider, *Nonviolent Action: What Christian Ethics Demands but Most Christians Have Never Really Tried* (Grand Rapids: Brazos, 2015), xv.

42. Walter Wink, *The Powers That Be: Theology for a New Millennium* (New York: Harmony, 1999), 100.

43. See Sider, *Nonviolent Action*; Preston Sprinkle with Andrew Rillera, *Nonviolence: The Revolutionay Way of Jesus*, rev. ed. (Colorado Springs: David C. Cook, 2021); Peter Ackerman and Jack DuVall, *A Force More Powerful: A Century of Non-Violent Conflict* (New York: St. Martin's Griffin, 2000).

## Chapter Five

1. Dietrich Bonhoeffer, *Ethics* (Minneapolis: Fortress, 2015), 81–103.

2. Bonhoeffer, *Ethics*, 94.

3. Bonhoeffer, *Ethics*, 96.

4. Bonhoeffer, *Ethics*, 97.

5. Jesse T. Jackson, "Matt Chandler's Deconstruction Comment Unravels Twitter," *ChurchLeaders* (blog), December 7, 2021, https://churchleaders.com/news/412115-matt-chandler-deconstruction-comment-unravels-twitter.html.

6. Kevin Deyoung, "It's Time for a New Culture War Strategy," *The Gospel Coalition* (blog), accessed October 18, 2022, https://www.thegospelcoalition.org/blogs/kevin-deyoung/its-time-for-a-new-culture-war-strategy/.

7. For more on this, see Martin E. Marty, *The Mystery of the Child* (Grand Rapids: Eerdmans, 2007).

8. Esau McCaulley, *Reading While Black: African Amer-*

*ican Biblical Interpretation as an Exercise in Hope* (Downers Grove, IL: IVP Academic, 2020), 68–69.

9. Jerry A. Pattengale, Todd C. Ream, and Christopher J. Devers, *Public Intellectuals and the Common Good: Christian Thinking for Human Flourishing* (Downers Grove, IL: IVP Academic, 2021), ix–x.

10. https://www.ccpubliclife.org/who-we-are.

11. "Former Obama Faith Adviser Launches Christian Political Organization," accessed October 19, 2022, https://news.yahoo.com/former-obama-faith-adviser-launches-christian-political-organization-150107664.html.

12. https://twitter.com/KeithSimon_/status/16026 63257218629634.

13. Kevin Dorst, "What Is Polarization?," *Reasonably Polarized*, September 18, 2020, https://www.psychology today.com/us/blog/reasonably-polarized/202009/what-is-polarization.

14. https://www.pewresearch.org/fact-tank/2016/01/12/presidential-job-approval-ratings-from-ike-to-obama/.

15. Rebecca Konyndyk DeYoung, *Glittering Vices: A New Look at the Seven Deadly Sins and Their Remedies*, 2nd ed. (Grand Rapids: Brazos, 2020), 42.

16. Dallas Willard, *The Divine Conspiracy: Rediscovering Our Hidden Life in God* (San Francisco: Harper, 1998), 147–48.

17. Willard, *The Divine Conspiracy*, 151.

18. George M. Marsden, foreword in Pattengale, Ream, and Devers, *Public Intellectuals and the Common Good*, ix.

19. Bonhoeffer, *Ethics*, 134.

20. Lawrence B. Finer et al., "Reasons U.S. Women Have Abortions: Quantitative and Qualitative Perspectives," *Perspectives on Sexual and Reproductive Health* 37, no. 3 (2005): 110–18.

21. The following is adapted from my article "Pro-Life for All Human Life," Christian Research Institute, https://www .equip.org/article/the-meaning-of-the-term-pro-life-a-point -counterpoint-conversation-pro-life-for-all-human-life/.

22. Scott Klusendorf, "The Case for Life," https://prolife training.com/resources/the-case-for-life/.

23. Alan Shlemon, "The S.L.E.D. Test," Stand to Reason, March 13, 2014, https://www.str.org/w/the-sled-test.

24. Gustav Ohler, *Theology of the Old Testament*, 2nd ed. (New York: Funk and Wagnalls, 1884), 145–46.

25. Data from the Guttmacher Institute, https://www.gutt macher.org/united-states/abortion#.

26. Death Penalty Information Center, https://deathpen altyinfo.org/policy-issues/innocence.

27. Death Penalty Information Center, https://deathpen altyinfo.org/policy-issues/race.

28. Brentin Mock, "Police Are More Aggressive Overall in Encounters with African Americans," Bloomberg, November 17, 2015, https://www.bloomberg.com/news/articles /2015-11-17/african-americans-are-subjected-to-non-fatal-use -of-police-force-than-whites.

29. Adolfo Flores, "More Immigrant Children Are Dying at the Border as the Trump Administration Sends People Back to Mexico," BuzzFeed, September 19, 2019, updated September 20, 2019, https://www.buzzfeednews.com/article/adol foflores/immigrant-children-dying-united-states-mexico -trump.

30. Molly Hennessy-Fiske, "Six Migrant Children Have Died in U.S. Custody. Here's What We Know about Them," *Los Angeles Times*, May 24, 2019, https://www.latimes.com/na tion/la-na-migrant-child-border-deaths-20190524-story.html.

31. Dara Lind and Lomi Kriel, "ICE Is Making Sure Kids Don't Have COVID-19—Then Expelling Them to 'Prevent the Spread' of COVID-19," ProPublica, August 10, 2020, https://www.propublica.org/article/ice-is-making-sure-migrant-kids-dont-have-covid-19-then-expelling-them-to-prevent-the-spread-of-covid-19.

32. See Dara Lind, "The Horrifying Conditions Facing Kids in Border Detention, Explained," Vox, June 25, 2019, https://www.vox.com/policy-and-politics/2019/6/25/18715725/children-border-detention-kids-cages-immigration; Lyndon Haviland, "Nielsen Resignation Doesn't Change Fact Child Sexual Abuse at Border Is Real Emergency," *USA Today*, April 9, 2019, https://www.usatoday.com/story/opinion/2019/04/09/immigrant-children-sexual-abuse-detention-centers-real-emergency-trump-column/3399019002/; Jim Sergent, Elizabeth Lawrence, Elinor Aspegren, and Olivia Sanchez, "Chilling First-Hand Reports of Migrant Detention Centers Highlight Smell of 'Urine, Feces,' Overcrowded Conditions," *USA Today*, July 16, 2019, https://www.usatoday.com/in-depth/news/politics/elections/2019/07/16/migrant-detention-centers-described-2019-us-government-accounts/1694638001/?_ga=2.34345447.711389776.1597090056-1334174796.1597090056.

33. Jennifer Ludden, "Undercover Video Targets Planned Parenthood," NPR, July 15, 2015, https://www.npr.org/sections/thetwo-way/2015/07/15/423212004/undercover-video-targets-planned-parenthood.

34. bell hooks, *All About Love: New Visions* (New York: William Morrow, 2018), xix.

35. bell hooks, *All About Love*, 19.

36. Thomas R. Yoder Neufeld, "'The God of Peace Will

Soon Crush Satan under Your Feet': Violence in the Gospel of Peace?," in *The Gospel of Peace in a Violent World: Christian Nonviolence for Communal Flourishing*, ed. Shawn Graves and Marlena Graves (Downers Grove, IL: IVP Academic, 2022), 65–66.

### Chapter Six

1. Search for the playlist "Memento Mori" by mike.austin-12 on Spotify if you want to check out the playlist.

2. Timothy D. Neufeld, *U2: Rock 'n' Roll to Change the World* (Lanham, MD: Rowman & Littlefield, 2018), 97.

3. U2 and Neil McCormick, *U2 by U2* (New York: It Books, 2006), 295–96.

4. Marlena Graves, *The Way Up Is Down: Becoming Yourself by Forgetting Yourself* (Downers Grove, IL: IVP, 2020), ch. 8.

5. Robert C. Roberts, *Spiritual Emotions: A Psychology of Christian Virtues* (Grand Rapids: Eerdmans, 2007), 123.

6. U2 and McCormick, *U2 by U2*, 6.

7. Thomas Merton, *Thoughts in Solitude* (New York: Farrar, Straus, and Giroux, 1958), 46.

# Selected Bibliography

Ackerman, Peter, and Jack DuVall. *A Force More Powerful: A Century of Non-Violent Conflict*. New York: St. Martin's Griffin, 2000.

Austin, Michael W. "Anger, Humility, and Civil Discourse." Pages 115–24 in *Righteous Indignation: Christian Philosophical and Theological Perspectives on Anger*. Edited by Gregory L. Bock and Court D. Lewis. Lanham, MD: Fortress Academic, 2021.

———. *God and Guns in America*. Grand Rapids: Eerdmans, 2020.

———. *Humility and Human Flourishing: A Study in Analytic Moral Theology*. Oxford: Oxford University Press, 2018.

Bacote, Vincent. "Drawing from the Well: Learning from African American Christian Formation." Pages 92–103 in *Tending Soul, Mind, and Body: The Art and Science of Spiritual Formation*. Edited by Gerald Hiestand and Todd Wilson. Downers Grove, IL: IVP Academic, 2019.

Barton, Ruth Haley. *Invitation to Solitude and Silence*. Downers Grove, IL: IVP, 2010.

Bates, Matthew W. *Salvation by Allegiance Alone: Rethinking Faith, Works, and the Gospel of Jesus the King*. Grand Rapids: Baker Academic, 2017.

Bonhoeffer, Dietrich. *Ethics*. Minneapolis: Fortress, 2015.

———. *Life Together*. Minneapolis: Fortress, 2015.

Burridge, Richard A. *Imitating Jesus: An Inclusive Approach to New Testament Ethics*. Grand Rapids: Eerdmans, 2007.

Chittister, Sister Joan. *Becoming Fully Human: The Greatest Glory of God*. Lanham, MD: Sheed & Ward, 2005.

DeYoung, Rebecca Konyndyk. "Courage." Pages 154–68 in *Being Good*, edited by Michael W. Austin and R. Douglas Geivett. Grand Rapids: Eerdmans, 2012.

———. *Glittering Vices: A New Look at the Seven Deadly Sins and Their Remedies*, 2nd ed. Grand Rapids: Brazos, 2020.

DeYoung, Rebecca Konyndyk, Colleen McCluskey, and Christina Van Dyke, *Aquinas's Ethics: Metaphysical Foundations, Moral Theory, and Theological Context*. Notre Dame: University of Notre Dame Press, 2009.

Foster, Richard J. *Celebration of Discipline*. San Francisco: HarperSanFrancisco, 1990.

Geivett, R. Douglas. "Forgiveness." Pages 204–41 in *Being Good*, edited by Michael W. Austin and R. Douglas Geivett. Grand Rapids: Eerdmans, 2012.

Graves, Marlena. *The Way Up Is Down: Becoming Yourself by Forgetting Yourself*. Downers Grove, IL: IVP, 2020.

Hays, Katie. *God Gets Everything God Wants*. Grand Rapids: Eerdmans, 2021.

Hildebrand, Dietrich von. *Humility: Wellspring of Virtue*. Manchester, NH: Sophia Institute Press, 1997.

hooks, bell. *All about Love: New Visions*. New York: William Morrow, 2018.

Kreglinger, Gisela H. *The Spirituality of Wine*. Grand Rapids: Eerdmans, 2016.

Lewis, C. S. *Mere Christianity*. San Francisco: HarperOne, 2015.

McCaulley, Esau. *Reading While Black: African American Biblical Interpretation as an Exercise in Hope*. Downers Grove, IL: IVP Academic, 2020.

Marty, Martin E. *The Mystery of the Child*. Grand Rapids: Eerdmans, 2007.

Mattison, William C., III. *Introducing Moral Theology: True Happiness and the Virtues*. Grand Rapids: Brazos, 2008.

Merton, Thomas. *Thoughts in Solitude*. New York: Farrar, Straus, and Giroux, 1958.

Miller, Christian. *The Character Gap: How Good Are We?* New York: Oxford University Press, 2017.

Murray, Andrew. *Humility: The Journey toward Holiness*. Minneapolis: Bethany House, 2001.

Myers, David G. "Humility: Psychology Meets Theology." *Reformed Review* 48 (1995): 195–206.

Nouwen, Henri J. M. *The Return of the Prodigal Son: A Story of Homecoming*. New York: Doubleday, 1992.

Padilla, C. René. *What Is Integral Mission?* Minneapolis: Fortress, 2021.

Pieper, Josef. *The Four Cardinal Virtues*. Translated by Richard Winston et al. Notre Dame: University of Notre Dame Press, 1966.

Sider, Ronald J. *Nonviolent Action: What Christian Ethics Demands but Most Christians Have Never Really Tried.* Grand Rapids: Brazos, 2015.

Sprinkle, Preston, with Andrew Rillera. *Nonviolence: The Revolutionay Way of Jesus.* Rev. ed. Colorado Springs: David C. Cook, 2021.

Teresa of Ávila. *Interior Castle or The Mansions.* Translated by E. Allison Peers. Radford, VA: Wilder, 2008.

Thomas à Kempis. *The Imitation of Christ.* Translated by William Creasy. Macon, GA: Mercer University Press, 2015.

Tisby, Jemar. *The Color of Compromise: The Truth about the American Church's Complicity in Racism.* Grand Rapids: Zondervan, 2019.

Willard, Dallas. *The Allure of Gentleness: Defending the Faith in the Manner of Jesus.* New York: HarperOne, 2015.

———. *The Divine Conspiracy: Rediscovering Our Hidden Life in God.* San Francisco: Harper, 1998.

———. *Life without Lack: Living in the Fullness of Psalm 23.* Nashville: Thomas Nelson, 2018.

———. *Renovation of the Heart: Putting on the Character of Christ.* Colorado Springs: NavPress, 2002.

———. *The Spirit of the Disciplines: Understanding How God Changes Lives.* San Francisco: HarperSanFrancisco, 1988.

Wink, Walter. *The Powers That Be: Theology for a New Millennium.* New York: Harmony, 1999.

Yoder Neufeld, Thomas R. "'The God of Peace Will Soon Crush Satan under Your Feet': Violence in the Gospel of Peace?" Pages 58–75 in *The Gospel of Peace in a Vio-*

*lent World: Christian Nonviolence for Communal Flour-ishing*. Edited by Shawn Graves and Marlena Graves. Downers Grove, IL: IVP Academic, 2022.

Zahn, Gordon C. *In Solitary Witness: The Life and Death of Franz Jägerstätter*. Boston: Beacon, 1968.

# Subject Index

# Subject Index

nonviolence, 111, 120, 122–25, 146
Norris, Kathleen, 167
Nouwen, Henri, 85, 175, 185

oppression, 43, 77, 112, 115, 123, 125, 131, 137
other-centeredness, 52, 54, 64

Padilla, René, 103
patience, 14, 53, 91, 94, 111
Paul, 26, 30–32, 38–41, 43, 51–52, 56, 94, 128
peace, 14, 27, 62, 74, 111–13, 133, 136, 165
peacemaking, 111–14, 136–37
perseverance, 161–62
pleasure, 1–2, 11, 27, 56, 70–71, 99
polarization, 67, 120, 141–46
politics, 1, 5, 41, 67, 81, 90, 122, 134–36, 140, 145
poverty, 84, 94, 129, 149
prayer: centering prayer, 106; the Lord's Prayer, 24, 72, 98; as a spiritual discipline, 18, 34, 74, 87, 93, 100–103; and U2, 158
prejudice, 77, 90
pride: according to Augustine, 17; in the author's life, 21, 44, 98; in community, 52; and false humility, 34; the forms of, 64–68; in the parable of the prodigal son, 84; the vice of, 23, 32, 42, 45, 54, 58, 90, 94, 105, 110, 124–25, 165

racism, 15, 113, 115, 119, 148, 154
repentance, 73, 84, 131
resentment, 73
respect, 1, 28, 31, 99, 119, 123, 140, 150
rest, 3, 11, 26, 36, 41, 47–48, 69, 78–79, 89, 115–18

righteousness, 1, 44, 101, 132–33, 136

self-centeredness, 84, 110, 131
self-control, 14, 20, 54, 56, 69–72
selfishness, 17, 36, 63, 80, 90
shalom, 3, 23, 37, 46
shame, 16, 146, 162
silence, 18, 34, 87, 106–8
sloth, 54, 64, 77–80, 82, 143–46, 155
solitude, 18, 87, 104–8
soul, 6, 26, 52, 76, 102, 133, 144–46, 157, 160
study, 74, 87, 96, 118, 123
suffering: and alcohol, 65; for Christ, 28, 89, 159, 161–62; Christ's example, 122; and compassion, 14, 54, 59, 61; and courage, 75–77; and pride, 42; and race, 111, 114–17, 137, 150; and war, 152

temptation, 16–17, 106, 163
Tisby, Jemar, 116–17
trauma, 148, 152
trials, 95, 159, 161
Trinity, 20, 33, 36, 47, 54, 90, 95

unity, 21, 23, 28, 41, 53, 75, 90–95, 114, 120, 124, 144

vainglory, 64, 143–44, 172

wealth, 1–2, 11, 27, 32, 42, 56, 62, 68, 94, 116, 151
Willard, Dallas, 6, 15, 88–89, 107
wisdom, 54, 56–58, 62, 65, 98, 117–18, 125, 140
wokeness, 132
worship, 91, 117

# *Scripture Index*